I0605064

Count Your Blessings

Publications International, Ltd.

Scripture quotations from *The Holy Bible, King James Version*

Images from Shutterstock.com

Louis Weber, CEO
Publications International, Ltd.
8140 Lehigh Avenue
Morton Grove, IL 60053

ISBN: 978-1-63938-867-7

Manufactured in China.

8 7 6 5 4 3 2 1

And God blessed them, and God said unto them, Be fruitful, and multiply, and replenish the earth, and subdue it: and have dominion over the fish of the sea, and over the fowl of the air, and over every living thing that moveth upon the earth.

Genesis 1:28

Work itself is a blessing. From the beginning, we had both the responsibility and privilege to be partners in God's plan. Fruitfulness is one of the joys we experience as we multiply and replenish. So this year, enjoy your various roles as a steward of God's creation.

Thou wilt keep him in perfect peace, whose mind is stayed on thee: because he trusteth in thee.

Isaiah 26:3

As you meditate on God's goodness to you and trust him for your daily provision, he will give you perfect peace. Nothing calms us like reflecting on his mercy and grace. Pause and worship; he is keeping you and caring for you today.

And ye shall serve the Lord your God, and he shall bless thy bread, and thy water; and I will take sickness away from the midst of thee.

Exodus 23:25

As we serve the God of heaven we find the things that matter are from his hand. Our health and our daily bread come from him—even a glass of water. Count your blessings today, and praise him.

The Lord bless thee, and keep thee: The Lord make his face shine upon thee, and be gracious unto thee: The Lord lift up his countenance upon thee, and give thee peace.

Numbers 6:24–26

This famous benediction, the Aaronic blessing, reminds you that a gracious God blesses you, keeps you, and gives you peace. May his face shine on you today. Remember, he is watching over you. And smiling.

Surely goodness and mercy shall follow me all the days of my life: and I will dwell in the house of the Lord forever.

Psalm 23:6

The goodness and mercy of God doesn't just hang out in the background of our days. It "follows" us. The word here actually has the sense of pursuing us, with intention and persistence. If you reflect on your life, this is likely true. He has helped you when you didn't deserve helping. That's the mercy. And he has blessed you when you didn't deserve blessing. That's the goodness. This is the nature of our God: to pursue us even when we are unaware or inattentive. And he does this all the days of our life, so we can dwell in his house forever.

And he will love thee, and bless thee, and multiply thee: he will also bless the fruit of thy womb, and the fruit of thy land, thy corn, and thy wine, and thine oil, the increase of thy kine, and the flocks of thy sheep, in the land which he sware unto thy fathers to give thee.

Deuteronomy 7:13

God gives us a place. And he promises to bless us and sustain us, increasing our fruit and blessing our efforts. More than that, he promises to love us. This is the greatest blessing of all.

When we fill our days with the noisy blur of constant activity, we miss the gifts and blessings of silence and stillness. Only by purposely taking the time to do nothing can we cultivate the inner wisdom and guidance we seek. It's in the quiet that we renew our connection to the source of inspiration, energy, and enthusiasm. Silence is more than golden. It's essential to a life well lived.

So that we may boldly say, The Lord is my helper, and I will not fear what man shall do unto me.

Hebrews 13:6

True courage is in this: "The Lord is my helper." What a bold, amazing truth. Because it is true, we don't need to be afraid of others' strength or even our own weakness. This confidence affects how we pray and how we live. This is not just confidence for the night, but for the day, at work or school or anywhere we go. We can boldly say "the Lord is my helper." We can boldly live it. What can anyone do to us, if the Lord is our helper?

O taste and see that the Lord is good: blessed is the man that trusteth in him.

Psalm 34:8

Oh Lord, may your presence today be more necessary and satisfying than good food. You are my soul's great need. I delight in both what you provide and who you are. What a blessing to know you and to trust you!

Bless the children, God of little ones, with their giggles and wide-eyed awe, their awaking assumption that today will be chock-full of surprises, learning, and love. Neither missing nor wasting a minute, they take nothing for granted, a message that blesses us. Remind us to go and do likewise.

And I will make of thee a great nation, and I will bless thee, and make thy name great; and thou shalt be a blessing.

Genesis 12:2

Lord, prosperity and posterity are both blessings from you. Help me today to see a hug from a grandchild or a quiet moment in a coffee shop as something you are doing that may impact many generations. Help me hear your voice and do your will. Make me a blessing.

Bless the Lord, O my soul, and forget not all his benefits.

Psalm 103:2

Remember all his benefits. Whether it's watching a flower unfolding in the morning sun, getting an occasional smile from a grumpy teen, or hearing from an old friend, it's good to list these blessings. And to thank God for them.

Lord, it's hard to count your blessings when all around you is chaos and despair. Though my heart is heavy and my mind cluttered, please help me to realize that before a flower can show its beauty to the sun, it first is a seed buried in the dirt. Help me to stand above the negative things in life and cast my eyes instead upon the positives that are always there, like the seedling, growing toward the moment when it will appear above ground, face to the sun.

The blessing of the Lord, it maketh rich, and he addeth no sorrow with it.

Proverbs 10:22

Real wealth isn't about money. It's about joy. Consider God's blessings today and move beyond your sorrow into the fullness of his presence and blessing. He will make you rich in matters of the heart and give you great gladness. Perhaps even a song.

A chart of my efforts to change traces
a jagged course, Lord, like the lines on
a heart-rate monitor. Reassure me that
instead of measuring my failures, ups
and downs mean simply that I am alive
and ever-changing. Help me become
consistent, but deliver me from flat lines.

Blessed are the meek: for they shall inherit the earth.

Matthew 5:5

Meek people don't envy or retaliate; instead, they are patient. And kind. No matter what happens they trust God's plan and purpose for their lives. Such people, free from anger and bitterness, are truly blessed.

Then believed they his words;
they sang his praise.

Psalm 106:12

After God parted the Red Sea and delivered his people from Pharaoh, it was then that they believed his words. It doesn't have to be this way, of course. We could just believe, but it's easier when we begin to count our blessing and recall his deliverance from our sin and its consequences. That's even more amazing than parting the Red Sea. When we make that connection, we will also sing his praises.

For I know the thoughts that I think toward you, saith the Lord, thoughts of peace, and not of evil, to give you an expected end.

Jeremiah 29:11

We can not begin to comprehend all God knows and understands. But this is what he thinks of you today: thoughts of peace. He wants to give you an expected end, but its not the end you expect. It's the one he expects. And it's very good.

It is of the Lord's mercies that we are not consumed, because his compassions fail not. They are new every morning: great is thy faithfulness.

Lamentations 3:22–23

We deserve much less than we get, yet his compassions fail not. Each morning welcomes new mercies and each day our blessings multiply. As you count them today, count his faithfulness—it is the greatest of them all.

I will abundantly bless her provision:
I will satisfy her poor with bread.

Psalm 132:15

Who is the "her" here? In this case it is Zion, the place where God dwells forever. It is the place where his people assemble to praise and worship him. It is the community of faith, the church of the living God. He will provide for his people, referred to in both the Old and New Testament as his bride. He will satisfy her hunger and meet her needs. And he will do so abundantly.

My Creator, blessed is your presence. For you and you alone give me power to walk through dark valleys into the light again. You and you alone give me hope when there seems no end to my suffering. You and you alone give me peace when the noise of my life overwhelms me. I ask that you give this same power, hope, and peace to all who know discouragement, that they, too, may be emboldened and renewed by your everlasting love. Amen.

Blessed are they which do hunger and thirst after righteousness: for they shall be filled.

Matthew 5:6

Jesus is the bread we really long for, and he graciously blesses us with his righteousness, filling us with spiritual nourishment and living water. Take a sip, today. No, take a long gulp and be completely satisfied.

The angel of the Lord encampeth round about them that fear him, and delivereth them.

Psalm 34:7

Angels do a lot of things. They bring messages and fight demons, for example. But for most of us, the most important thing they do is guard us and protect us. Be comforted by this: your awe of God results in his ministering spirits and heavenly hosts protecting you, all according to his mercy and care. These guardians are the angels of the Lord.

But this I say, He which soweth sparingly shall reap also sparingly; and he which soweth bountifully shall reap also bountifully.

2 Corinthians 9:6

In discussing their giving to the Lord's work, the Apostle Paul tells the church in Corinth to give regularly and cheerfully. He also tells them to give generously. If they sow bountifully, they will reap bountifully. It is pretty clear we can't outgive God, whose resources and generosity are infinitely greater than our own. So don't be stingy, especially when it comes to Kingdom purposes.

But seek ye first the kingdom of God, and his righteousness; and all these things shall be added unto you.

Matthew 6:33

"All these things" is a lot. Jesus is speaking of our daily needs, but there is more. Those provisions are in addition to his kingdom and his righteousness. Oh Lord, help me to seek you first. And to receive your blessings with gratitude.

Give, and it shall be given unto you; good measure, pressed down, and shaken together, and running over, shall men give into your bosom. For with the same measure that ye mete withal it shall be measured to you again.

Luke 6:38

We should be generous to others because God is generous to us. Grace is an aspect of his character. But others are more generous when we are more generous, when we are more like him. Who can you bless today?

The thief cometh not, but for to steal, and to kill, and to destroy: I am come that they might have life, and that they might have it more abundantly.

John 10:10

Abundant life is the blessing we should most treasure, and Christ came to give it to us. The life you have in him today is more abundant than you can imagine or comprehend. Count your blessings, if you can.

And we know that all things work together for good to them that love God, to them who are the called according to his purpose.

Romans 8:28

If you love God, you are called to his purpose. Embrace it, with the full assurance that everything you encounter today will work out for his glory and for your good. What a blessing this is, to be partners in his plan.

But my God shall supply all your need according to his riches in glory by Christ Jesus.

Philippians 4:19

Increase Mather, a Puritan pastor, said “The blessings of heaven are never exhausted, no matter how much we draw from them.” That’s true, because through Christ, God meets all your needs according to his limitless riches. Praise him.

I remember being told to give thanks in advance for things I wished to see in my life. I thought that was strange, but decided to try it. Interestingly, putting myself in a state of gratitude changed not only my attitude, but the energy I was giving off. Sure enough, doors began to open and people began to respond to me differently.

When I am thankful for what I have it seems to move energy back in my favor. Sharing those blessings opens even bigger doors, to happiness and a sense of joy and wonder.

Every good gift and every perfect gift is from above, and cometh down from the Father of lights, with whom is no variableness, neither shadow of turning.

James 1:17

Every good and perfect gift is from God. And we should receive them with gratitude and joy. But the unchanging God is the most perfect gift of all. He doesn't vary or turn, and gives us light that never even flickers. Be in awe.

And God is able to make all grace abound toward you; that ye, always having all sufficiency in all things, may abound to every good work.

2 Corinthians 9:8

All sufficiency in all things. What more could we want or need? By God's power, such grace abounds toward you and through you. The Puritan author William Burnall wrote, "The blessings of God are like the sun: sufficient for all, yet shining uniquely upon each."

And let us not be weary in well doing: for in due season we shall reap, if we faint not.

Galatians 6:9

Don't faint. Seriously, don't give up or draw back. Don't quit doing good. There is a harvest to reap and thanksgiving to come. You will be blessed and so will others, all in due season.

Now unto him that is able to do exceeding abundantly above all that we ask or think, according to the power that worketh in us. Unto him be glory in the church by Christ Jesus throughout all ages, world without end.

Ephesians 3:20–21

God can do more than we can ask or imagine. Abundantly more. This is the power of our great God. And that power is at work in us. His power is the blessing you need today.

Be careful for nothing; but in every thing by prayer and supplication with thanksgiving let your requests be made known unto God.

Philippians 4:6

In prayer, we worship God, ask for what we truly need, and even things we don't need. Then we thank him for his multiple and gracious gifts. He hears us. He knows us. He loves us. He sorts it all out and blesses us. So, why worry?

Therefore God give thee of the dew of heaven, and the fatness of the earth, and plenty of corn and wine.

Genesis 27:28

Oh Lord, help me see your grace in ordinary things, the scent of a flower or the song of a bird. Help me enjoy the food your provide, and to see it as coming from your good and gracious hand. May I delight in all your gifts today. Especially the little ones.

Blessed is the man that endureth temptation: for when he is tried, he shall receive the crown of life, which the Lord hath promised to them that love him.

James 1:12

We receive many blessings by God's grace, but none greater than the crown of life, both in this life and the life to come. So, receive and anticipate this crown today as you resist temptation. And remember, it's easier if you love him. Guaranteed.

And he poured the anointing oil upon Aaron's head and anointed him, to sanctify him.

Leviticus 8:12

To be anointed in God's love is to be made into a powerful force for good. Be strong and go forward spreading light and love, for the world needs both now more than ever!

A healthy friendship enhances our lives. What a blessing to have someone who wants to share all our joys and sorrows. We should continually strive to be the kind of friend God would like us to be—and the kind of friend that we would like to have.

Blessed shalt thou be when thou comest in, and blessed shalt thou be when thou goest out.

Deuteronomy 28:6

Thank you, Lord, for blessing me all the time, both when I come in and when I go out. I'm grateful that I experience this in all places and times, at work, at church, or at home. Your blessings are constant and sufficient.

And it came to pass from the time that he had made him overseer in his house, and over all that he had, that the Lord blessed the Egyptian's house for Joseph's sake; and the blessing of the Lord was upon all that he had in the house, and in the field.

Genesis 39:5

The blessings God gives us spill over into the lives of those around us. Never underestimate the ways his gifts are multiplied, enriching those we love and those we serve. May the Lord make you a blessing today.

And the Lord passed by before him, and proclaimed, The Lord, The Lord God, merciful and gracious, longsuffering, and abundant in goodness and truth.

Exodus 34:6

As you count your blessings today, count these: God's mercy, grace, patience, goodness and truth. And that he reveals himself to you. Catherine of Siena said, "Thank you, Lord, for blessing me with the grace to know and love you. May I always remain in your favor."

Then I will give you rain in due season, and the land shall yield her increase, and the trees of the field shall yield their fruit.

Leviticus 26:4

Lord, thanks for all you do in "due season." Your timing is perfect, and I get the rain and the fruit I need, exactly when I need it. Today, remind me that your blessings are always just on time.

If I'm honest with myself, I'll admit that the greatest joys in my life have sprung from the fertile grounds of suffering—but only after I have asked God to take charge of my garden of sorrow.

For thou, Lord, wilt bless the righteous; with favour wilt thou compass him as with a shield.

Psalm 5:12

God's favor is not a parking spot next to the store, or a pay increase at work. Those are blessings, of course, unless you actually need to exercise. His favor is his grace, and it is primarily spiritual. It starts with salvation and includes peace, joy, strength, wisdom—anything you need today to know and do God's will.

As for God, his way is perfect; the word of the Lord is tried: he is a buckler to all them that trust in him.

2 Samuel 22:31

Be glad today that the word of the Lord is tried, and not tired. Always fresh and always perfect, may his word protect you and nourish you today. His word is your shield and your sure defense.

Blessed be the Lord, that hath given rest unto his people Israel, according to all that he promised: there hath not failed one word of all his good promise, which he promised by the hand of Moses his servant.

1 Kings 8:56

Lord, you promised to give me peace in Christ. Help me cease my striving and rest in your promise. Not a single word of it will fail. So when the baby cries or my coworker complains, remind me of your faithfulness and give me rest.

And Jabez called on the God of Israel, saying, Oh that thou wouldest bless me indeed, and enlarge my coast, and that thine hand might be with me, and that thou wouldest keep me from evil, that it may not grieve me! And God granted him that which he requested.

1 Chronicles 4:10

Lord, enlarge my coast today. Give me more ways to help and bless others, increasing my opportunities and multiplying my efforts. Keep me from evil—mine or others—as I serve you. Be with me. And bless me indeed.

And in that day ye shall ask me nothing. Verily, verily, I say unto you, Whatsoever ye shall ask the Father in my name, he will give it you.

John 16:23

What does it mean to ask the Father in Jesus's name? What does it mean that "He will give it to you"? We can all think of times we've asked for things and didn't get a response. Clearly, we've asked for a lot of stuff, and he didn't give it to us. Mercifully, he says no some of the time. Or not yet. Graciously, he even often says yes and we still want more. But is that what this promise is about? No. It's about his name. It's about his purpose and his reputation. Whatever we ask that's about his Kingdom, or his glory, he will always give us that.

Thou wilt shew me the path of life: in thy presence is fulness of joy; at thy right hand there are pleasures for evermore.

Psalm 16:11

Gracious Father, show me the path of life today. May I experience real joy as I anticipate eternal pleasures, taking each step of the way in faith and obedience. You are good to me and good for me. I praise your name.

The liberal soul shall be made fat: and he that watereth shall be watered also himself.

Proverbs 11:25

Help me, Lord, to be a generous soul, one whose spirit and provision spills out into my world. You pour back into me what I pour out, refreshing both friends and strangers.

And therefore will the Lord wait, that he may be gracious unto you, and therefore will he be exalted, that he may have mercy upon you: for the Lord is a God of judgment: blessed are all they that wait for him.

Isaiah 30:18

Sometimes the blessings of God don't come when we want them to. We have to wait. When the blessing comes, however, we are more grateful because he is more gracious. And we praise him more.

For the Lord God is a sun and shield: the Lord will give grace and glory: no good thing will he withhold from them that walk uprightly.

Psalm 84:11

Lord, may I take the right steps today, seeing the path clearly because you are my light and fearing no evil because you are my shield. Grace and glory will go with me, and no good thing will I lack. I praise you.

Like the turkey wishbone, God of wholeness, I am being pulled apart by job, family, home, errands, friends, and my needs. I'm preoccupied with what I am not doing and feel the pull to do it all. Help me choose wisely. Remind me of all you have given me. Remind me, O God, to negotiate for a leaner lifestyle, for I am part of the pull. In the tugging days ahead, be the hinge that keeps my life's parts synchronized in harmonious movement, not split apart at all.

For your shame ye shall have double; and for confusion they shall rejoice in their portion: therefore in their land they shall possess the double: everlasting joy shall be unto them.

Isaiah 61:7

Lord, when I am excluded or embarrassed by others, please give me twice the joy of knowing you. Double the blessings I can count and assure me of your love. It is my dearest treasure.

So shall thy barns be filled with plenty, and thy presses shall burst out with new wine.

Proverbs 3:10

Abundance is the perfect word to describe your blessings, from the food and drink on your table to the joy and satisfaction of knowing God. As you count your blessings every day you will find them filled with plenty.

For ye shall go out with joy, and be led forth with peace: the mountains and the hills shall break forth before you into singing, and all the trees of the field shall clap their hands.

Isaiah 55:12

Among our chief blessings are God's joy and peace. Receive them today and you will then join all nature in singing. Find a worship song or old hymn and sing it out loud. Clap your hands and be glad.

And I will make them and the places round about my hill a blessing; and I will cause the shower to come down in his season; there shall be showers of blessing.

Ezekiel 34:26

Are you in a dry season? Has it been a while since you were able to laugh or delight in some small grace? The Lord is able to make you a blessing today. A shower of his blessings is all around. Lift your eyes to him and be refreshed.

What man is there of you, whom if his son ask bread, will he give him a stone? Or if he ask a fish, will he give him a serpent? If ye then, being evil, know how to give good gifts unto your children, how much more shall your Father which is in heaven give good things to them that ask him?

Matthew 7:9–11

Even someone who might be considered a bad father often wants to provide good things for his kids. He wants to remember their birthday or get them something for Christmas, even when he can't. Sometimes even a good dad is inconsistent or ineffective, because even the best dad is a mere shadow of our heavenly Father. We have a perfect Father in heaven who gives good things to his children. Remember his good and perfect gifts today.

She stretcheth out her hand to the poor; yea, she reacheth forth her hands to the needy.

Proverbs 31:20

My husband and I work hard, but some months money is tight. We have become adept at cutting costs, and although we will never be what our culture considers wealthy, I am grateful that we have what we need. The other day, I read about devastating flooding in Louisiana, and was reminded of how generosity can manifest itself in different ways. While we can donate a small amount of cash, I also, perhaps more crucially, can devote some of my time to volunteer efforts. I am healthy and can even donate blood. God, I am blessed in so many ways; please help me to remember the importance of generosity, and how it can take many forms.

For he shall be as a tree planted by the waters, and that spreadeth out her roots by the river, and shall not see when heat cometh, but her leaf shall be green; and shall not be careful in the year of drought, neither shall cease from yielding fruit.

Jeremiah 17:8

May I be rooted today in the reality of who you are, Lord. Make me fruitful, even in seasons of drought. You said you were the living water, dear Jesus. Water my soul, I pray.

He found him in a desert land, and in the waste howling wilderness; he led him about, he instructed him, he kept him as the apple of his eye.

Deuteronomy 32:10

This is our story. Like the ancient Hebrews, we too were wandering around in a wilderness, thirsty and lost, surrounded by noise and confusion. The winds howled and the sun beat down. But then God found us and led us. He taught us. And, beyond our expectation or merit, we became the object of his delight, his own sons and daughters. It's a great story, because it's true.

Bring ye all the tithes into the storehouse, that there may be meat in mine house, and prove me now herewith, saith the Lord of hosts, if I will not open you the windows of heaven, and pour you out a blessing, that there shall not be room enough to receive it.

Malachi 3:10

The windows of heaven open on those who are generous, to those who are cheerful givers. And the Lord is willing to prove that. He will pour out his blessings on those who give time, money or care to his work and to his people. For such, his grace overflows in abundance and joy.

Come unto me, all ye that labour and are heavy laden, and I will give you rest.

Matthew 11:28

Sometimes, the blessing we really need is a break, a pause in the stress of a busy season at work or home. Real rest is in Christ, if we just come to him. Let him carry your burdens today. Then take a deep breath and relax.

Lord, help me to depend on you to be my source of goodness. I don't always feel like being patient, kind, loving, or joyful, but you are all of these things by your very nature. So right now I place my strengths and weaknesses into your hands, asking you to infuse them with yourself and to make them instruments of good that will serve others for your sake.

Fear not, little flock; for it is your Father's good pleasure to give you the kingdom.

Luke 12:32

Such a tender image, to be a small lamb in the Father's kingdom. But that's reason enough to overcome our fears. He will provide for us and protect us. And it delights him to do so. Fear not, little flock.

Blessed be the God and Father of our Lord Jesus Christ, who hath blessed us with all spiritual blessings in heavenly places in Christ.

Ephesians 1:3

Lord, give me eyes to see spiritual blessings in heavenly places. So much of your goodness is beyond my ability to see or understand. Please give me a sense of awe today. Show me how great you are. And I will praise you.

Peace I leave with you, my peace I give unto you: not as the world giveth, give I unto you. Let not your heart be troubled, neither let it be afraid.

John 14:27

Dear God, everything around me seems to be falling apart. But don't let my heart be troubled. Don't let me be afraid. The world cannot equal the gift you give: peace with you and peace from you. Steady my heart with this, Lord. Steady my heart.

I have shewed you all things, how that so labouring ye ought to support the weak, and to remember the words of the Lord Jesus, how he said, It is more blessed to give than to receive.

Acts 20:35

Following the example of our Lord, we feel pleasure and purpose in helping the weak and being compassionate to those in need.

Bless us in this time of play together. Let each child know he or she is loved. And let us parents recognize that the love we offer here is the same affection you have already worked in our own hearts.

But as for you, ye thought evil against me; but God meant it unto good, to bring to pass, as it is this day, to save much people alive.

Genesis 50:20

Despite the designs of Joseph's brothers, God was working out a greater good. This is how he blesses us, even when the odds are stacked against us. Trust him today and wait for his plan to be revealed.

Honour thy father and thy mother: that thy days may be long upon the land which the Lord thy God giveth thee.

Exodus 20:12

You can honor your elderly parents today, even though you no longer have to obey them. So, pick up the phone or drive over to see them. You can make their day and please God at the same time.

*For what nation is there so great,
who hath God so nigh unto them,
as the Lord our God is in all things
that we call upon him for?*

Deuteronomy 4:7

God's presence with his people is blessing indeed. He is near us and in all things that pertain to us. We can call on him and he hears us. How blessed we are!

If I count the things I've asked for that you have not given me, I begin to believe you do not love me, God. But if, instead, I bring to mind all of the goodness you have shown me, I come to trust that you have never given me less than what I need and often have blessed me with far more from a depth of love I cannot comprehend.

And the Lord appeared unto him the same night, and said, I am the God of Abraham thy father: fear not, for I am with thee, and will bless thee, and multiply thy seed for my servant Abraham's sake.

Genesis 26:24

It is great blessing that the Lord shows up exactly when we need him. And his message is always the same: fear not, for I am with you. He will bless us and we will praise him.

And shewing mercy unto thousands of them that love me, and keep my commandments.

Exodus 20:6

You are not alone in your walk of faith. God's mercy is being shown to those all around you. Many are experiencing his blessing and keeping his commandments. Count faithful friends among your many blessings.

For I will have respect unto you, and make you fruitful, and multiply you, and establish my covenant with you.

Leviticus 26:9

This promise, which God makes to his people, is filled with the promises of a covenant-keeping God. He will honor your efforts to serve him. Be faithful. And be blessed.

(The Lord God of your fathers make you a thousand times so many more as ye are, and bless you, as he hath promised you!)

Deuteronomy 1:11

The blessings we receive as we believe God's promises cannot be counted. They are a thousand times greater than we expected, and are deeper than we knew. Count your blessings tonight instead of sheep. And rest in the goodness of God.

Change is never easy, but the blessings it bestows upon us are magnificent. Just ask the caterpillar struggling within the tight confines of a cocoon. Even as it struggles, it is becoming something glorious, something beautiful, soon to emerge as a winged butterfly. Change may bring temporary pain and discomfort, but it also brings the promise of a new life filled with joy and freedom and the ability to soar even higher than we ever did before.

Behold, I set before you this day a blessing and a curse; A blessing, if ye obey the commandments of the Lord your God, which I command you this day.

Deuteronomy 11:26–27

Lord, I have choices to make today. I want to choose blessing. Show me the way of obedience and blessing, loving you and loving my neighbor. This is the greatest commandment and the path of joy.

In that I command thee this day to love the Lord thy God, to walk in his ways, and to keep his commandments and his statutes and his judgments, that thou mayest live and multiply: and the Lord thy God shall bless thee in the land whither thou goest to possess it.

Deuteronomy 30:16

I love you, Father. That's what you really want. I may pass through some strange territory today, but you go before me and with me. Bless me, and I will be safe and fruitful, confident in your love.

Have not I commanded thee? Be strong and of a good courage; be not afraid, neither be thou dismayed: for the Lord thy God is with thee whithersoever thou goest.

Joshua 1:9

As I count my blessings today, Lord, I am most thankful for your comforting presence. Your spirit goes with me, giving me courage and strength. You are with me, and it gives me joy.

Therefore now let it please thee to bless the house of thy servant, that it may continue for ever before thee: for thou, O Lord God, hast spoken it: and with thy blessing let the house of thy servant be blessed for ever.

2 Samuel 7:29

Lord God, you have spoken. Your promises continue forever. May I see them in your word. And may I believe them. Bless me and bless my house, just as you promised.

Thine, O Lord, is the greatness, and the power, and the glory, and the victory, and the majesty: for all that is in the heaven and in the earth is thine; thine is the kingdom, O Lord, and thou art exalted as head above all.

1 Chronicles 29:11

Since all that is in heaven and all that is on the earth are yours, God, you will never run out of blessings. May I worship you today in all your power and glory, exalting you as head above all.

If my people, which are called by my name, shall humble themselves, and pray, and seek my face, and turn from their wicked ways; then will I hear from heaven, and will forgive their sin, and will heal their land.

2 Chronicles 7:14

Lord, revive your church. May your people seek you, with humility and repentance. Hear us. Forgive us. Heal us. This is the blessing we seek: to be called by your name and to see your face.

Then he said unto them, Go your way, eat the fat, and drink the sweet, and send portions unto them for whom nothing is prepared: for this day is holy unto our Lord: neither be ye sorry; for the joy of the Lord is your strength.

Nehemiah 8:10

It is a blessing to have what we need. It is a greater blessing to have enough to share. Ask God for the strength to joyfully share with others today. That will make it a holy day, any day of the week.

When the darkness casts shadows upon us
and the answers are nowhere in sight,
hope lifts us up on a wing and a prayer
and carries us back to the light.

So the Lord blessed the latter end of Job more than his beginning: for he had fourteen thousand sheep, and six thousand camels, and a thousand yoke of oxen, and a thousand she asses.

Job 42:12

After great loss we often experience great provision. It is never the same, but it is always sufficient. Wait for the blessing today, trusting the Father's heart.

The Lord also will be a refuge for the oppressed, a refuge in times of trouble.

Psalm 9:9

Are you mistreated, abused, neglected or alone? All of the above? God is a refuge for the oppressed. Seek the comfort of his presence and experience his blessing. He sees you and hears you. And he loves you.

God of all things, we thank you for all your creatures, from the largest to the smallest. In each of these wondrous animals, we see your creative touch. Help us respect all you have created, to protect their lives, and to be ready to learn from them anything you would like to teach us.

I will bless the Lord at all times: his praise shall continually be in my mouth.

Psalm 34:1

While God's blessings involve his generous provision of spiritual, physical, or emotional benefits, blessing God is our response of praise, gratitude, and reverence. He is generous at all times. So, bless the Lord at all times.

Bless this candlelit festival of birthday celebration, Lord, for our special loved one. Join us as we blow out candles and joke about setting the cake ablaze, about golden ages and silver hairs. Our laughter is bubbling up from gratitude that the years are only enriching this special celebrant. We are grateful that the years are also enriching our lives as friends and family as well, for we are the ones receiving the best birthday gift today: the gift of knowing this special person. Thank you for sharing.

The Lord is merciful and gracious, slow to anger, and plenteous in mercy.

Psalm 103:8

God's patience is a blessing. Whatever you are facing today, rejoice that God is slow to anger. He will graciously wait for you to catch up. He has plenty of mercy, more than enough for you on a bad day.

He that handleth a matter wisely shall find good: and whoso trusteth in the Lord, happy is he.

Proverbs 16:20

True blessing or happiness are the result of our faith in God's purposes, not our own plans. Yes, it is good to plan. It is better to trust God for the outcome. Confidence and peace are the blessing we really want.

And my people shall dwell in a peaceable habitation, and in sure dwellings, and in quiet resting places.

Isaiah 32:18

What a blessing is a peaceable place. Security and silence are often missing in our lives. Do you have a safe and silent place to go? Go there and thank God for it.

He's got you and me, brother, in his hands,
He's got you and me, sister, in his hands,
He's got all of us together in his hands,
He's got the whole world in his hands.

Gentle healers of mind, body, and spirit are surely a gift from you sent to travel lonely roads as our companions. Sustain them as they sustain us; they are a channel of your love.

And the Lord shall guide thee continually, and satisfy thy soul in drought, and make fat thy bones: and thou shalt be like a watered garden, and like a spring of water, whose waters fail not.

Isaiah 58:11

If you are experiencing a spiritual drought today, thirsting for the living water Christ promised, take heart. Call on him and he will satisfy you, guiding you continually and watering the garden of your soul.

The Lord hath appeared of old unto me, saying, Yea, I have loved thee with an everlasting love: therefore with lovingkindness have I drawn thee.

Jeremiah 31:3

Do you remember a time when the Lord assured you of his love? It is still true. His love is everlasting, and he is drawing you to himself. You may have changed, but he has not. Ask him to appear again.

Sow to yourselves in righteousness, reap in mercy; break up your fallow ground: for it is time to seek the Lord, till he come and rain righteousness upon you.

Hosea 10:12

Fallow ground is uncultivated and unplowed, hard and unfruitful. Some days our hearts are like that. But sow righteousness and seek the Lord. He will come and it will rain, making your heart soft and fertile again.

The Lord thy God in the midst of thee is mighty; he will save, he will rejoice over thee with joy; he will rest in his love, he will joy over thee with singing.

Zephaniah 3:17

The Lord is mighty to save and happy to do it. Make his heart glad today, delighting in his presence and resting in his love. Turn to him and he will start singing. This is the Father's heart.

Ask, and it shall be given you; seek, and ye shall find; knock, and it shall be opened unto you.

Matthew 7:7

God delights in answering your earnest prayer, Ask, seek, knock—these are the conditions for his will to be worked out in your life. Seek his will and the door will open to you.

And he took them up in his arms, put his hands upon them, and blessed them.

Mark 10:16

Jesus took the children in his arms and blessed them. With gentleness, he embraced them. He will do this for you too, because you are his child. And you are blessed.

And he lifted up his eyes on his disciples, and said, Blessed be ye poor: for yours is the kingdom of God.

Luke 6:20

To be poor is not to be impoverished, although you may be. This blessing is for those who are poor in spirit, humble and grateful, without any sense of entitlement or expectation. Is this your heart? Then you are blessed.

Jesus said unto her, I am the resurrection, and the life: he that believeth in me, though he were dead, yet shall he live.

John 11:25

Few blessings can exceed this: victory over death and hope of eternal life. This is the promise of Jesus, speaking to the sister of Lazarus and speaking to you as well. Believe in him and you will live.

Bless them which persecute you: bless, and curse not.

Romans 12:14

As God has blessed us, we are to bless others, even our enemies. Admittedly this is hard, but we have the perfect example in Christ and the perfect helper in his Spirit. Learn to do this, and your own blessings will increase.

But the fruit of the Spirit is love, joy, peace, longsuffering, gentleness, goodness, faith, meekness, temperance: against such there is no law.

Galatians 5:22–23

The Spirit of God has come to give us spiritual blessings, consistent and compelling virtues that change us and change our world. Which of these do you most need today? Ask the Spirit for his help and be a blessing.

For by grace are ye saved through faith; and that not of yourselves: it is the gift of God.

Ephesians 2:8

Grace is not only the source of our blessings; it is the ground of our salvation, a gift we cannot earn and a work we cannot do. This greatest of blessings is offered freely through faith. It is only a prayer away.

Being confident of this very thing, that he which hath begun a good work in you will perform it until the day of Jesus Christ.

Philippians 1:6

God's persistence is a blessing. He doesn't give up on us, chipping away at our hard hearts and drawing us to himself. This is his good work and the basis of our confidence. He will perform it, and we are blessed.

Let your conversation be without covetousness; and be content with such things as ye have: for he hath said, I will never leave thee, nor forsake thee.

Hebrews 13:5

Can you be content with the blessing you have received? There are more to come, but they are in God's purpose and plan. Resist covetousness, then, and be content. He will not leave you or forsake you.

Confess your faults one to another, and pray one for another, that ye may be healed. The effectual fervent prayer of a righteous man availeth much.

James 5:16

Answered prayer is a blessing. Restored relationships are another. Pray for peace in broken relationships and confess your own failures. But pray fervently, that you may be healed. Then remember this blessing—a friend or relative regained.

And God shall wipe away all tears from their eyes; and there shall be no more death, neither sorrow, nor crying, neither shall there be any more pain: for the former things are passed away.

Revelation 21:4

Lord, hasten the day when there will be no more tears. I long for your kingdom, for the passing of sadness and sorrow and the arrival of your perfect justice and joy. Bless me with a glimpse of this, Father. Give me hope.

And the Lord hath blessed my master greatly; and he is become great: and he hath given him flocks, and herds, and silver, and gold, and menservants, and maidservants, and camels, and asses.

Genesis 24:35

Lord, I am not asking you to give me all that you gave Abraham and his household. I have enough stuff already. But I am asking you to make me great in faith and obedience, a blessing to many and a faithful servant. Give me this.

The Lord is my strength and song, and he is become my salvation: he is my God, and I will prepare him an habitation; my father's God, and I will exalt him.

Exodus 15:2

Lord, be my strength and my song, You are my God and my salvation, so come and live in my heart as I exalt you. Help me prepare my heart for your Spirit and I will worship you.

Then I will command my blessing upon you in the sixth year, and it shall bring forth fruit for three years.

Leviticus 25:21

At God's command, the ancient Hebrews would give the land a "sabbath." But God said he would give a harvest in the sixth year sufficient for years seven and eight. If you obey him, he will bless you abundantly, too.

I am grateful, O God, that your standards run more to how we're loving you and one another than how we appear. If you judged on lawns, I would be out in the cold! Mine is the yard where kids gather. Ball games, sprinkler tag's muddy marathons, snow fort constructions, and bike repair—these all happen here. Thank you for my rutted, littered lawn. It's the most beautiful landscape, dotted as it is with children who will be grown and gone faster than we can say "replant."

But thou shalt remember the Lord thy God: for it is he that giveth thee power to get wealth, that he may establish his covenant which he sware unto thy fathers, as it is this day.

Deuteronomy 8:18

Your job, and the strength to do your job, are blessings from God. Remember that. This is one way he kept his promise to provide for parents and grandparents, and is keeping his promise to you. See your work as a blessing and give thanks.

O Lord, bless our life stages, for they read like growth rings on a mighty tree: our beginnings and firsts with their excitement, newness, and anxiety; our middles, full of diligence and commitment and, yes, we confess, sometimes boredom, but also risk and derring-do; our "nexts," the harvests and reapings; the slowing down and freedom. In your hands this time can be rich and full like an overflowing cup, not a last or a final or an empty or an ending stage at all. You are an Alpha and Omega God, the parentheses between which we live, move, and have our being. Bless our comings and goings.

There shall not any man be able to stand before thee all the days of thy life: as I was with Moses, so I will be with thee: I will not fail thee, nor forsake thee.

Joshua 1:5

Joshua is promised that no one will stand before him in battle. God will be with him, as he had been with Moses. As you fight for justice today, remember he is with you. He will not fail you or forsake you. You are not alone.

Only fear the Lord, and serve him in truth with all your heart: for consider how great things he hath done for you.

1 Samuel 12:24

Father God, help me serve you today with all my heart. Help me to remember all the great things you have done for me and will do for me. I am in awe of your greatness and your grace.

And it came to pass, when the vessels were full, that she said unto her son, Bring me yet a vessel. And he said unto her, There is not a vessel more. And the oil stayed.

2 Kings 4:6

As creditors threaten to take a widow's sons to settle her debts, Elisha tells a widow to fill every jar she has with oil from one small jar. She can then sell the oil, miraculously multiplied. You may need a miracle today. God is able.

And David said to Solomon his son, Be strong and of good courage, and do it: fear not, nor be dismayed: for the Lord God, even my God, will be with thee; he will not fail thee, nor forsake thee, until thou hast finished all the work for the service of the house of the Lord.

1 Chronicles 28:20

Father, help me finish the work I have started for you. Give me the courage and strength I need to serve you until the end, emboldened by your unfailing presence and love. I am not afraid, Lord, because you are with me.

Ye shall not need to fight in this battle: set yourselves, stand ye still, and see the salvation of the Lord with you, O Judah and Jerusalem: fear not, nor be dismayed; to morrow go out against them: for the Lord will be with you.

2 Chronicles 20:17

It is nice to know when to fight. And it is better to know when to wait. Help me stand still and see your work, Lord. And when it is time to go out, go with me and dispel my fear.

So we fasted and besought our God for this: and he was intreated of us.

Ezra 8:23

Fasting is one way God knows we are serious. Earnest seeking is another. He wants to be sought by us, and he wants to listen to us, and answer our need. This is his nature and our joy.

For thou hast made him most blessed for ever: thou hast made him exceeding glad with thy countenance.

Psalm 21:6

David is speaking to God, praising him for his blessings and favor. And David is talking about himself, about the joy he has as God smiles on him. God is smiling on you today. Be exceeding glad.

Oh how great is thy goodness, which thou hast laid up for them that fear thee; which thou hast wrought for them that trust in thee before the sons of men!

Psalm 31:19

Lord, right here, right now, in front of everyone, I want to celebrate how good you are. With reverence and awe, I want to praise you for every blessing. And I want to do it openly and joyfully.

Gratitude is an attitude of loving what you have, and this undoubtedly leads to having even more. When you open your eyes to the bountiful blessings already in your life, you realize just how abundant the world really is. Suddenly, you feel more giving, more loving, and more open to even greater blessings. Gratitude is a key that unlocks the door to treasures you already have, and it yields greater treasures yet to be discovered.

Praise ye the Lord. Blessed is the man that feareth the Lord, that delighteth greatly in his commandments.

Psalm 112:1

I will fear you today, Lord, and I will delight in your law. There is blessing in your presence and praise, as you come near to those who come near you. Draw me to yourself, Lord, and make me glad.

He that hath pity upon the poor lendeth unto the Lord; and that which he hath given will he pay him again.

Proverbs 19:17

The Lord notes the generosity of his people and repays them with his kindness and presence. He cares about those who have little, and he expects his people to care too. Be generous and be glad.

A faithful man shall abound with blessings: but he that maketh haste to be rich shall not be innocent.

Proverbs 28:20

We need faith more than we need money. God will bless us, providing for our needs, but greed leads to folly and to sin. So, be content and be blessed, trusting God and abounding with blessing.

Every man also to whom God hath given riches and wealth, and hath given him power to eat thereof, and to take his portion, and to rejoice in his labour; this is the gift of God.

Ecclesiastes 5:19

Your portion and your work are gifts from God, and they are sufficient. He gives you the money you need, and the good you need, and the strength you need. These gifts are blessing enough.

He giveth power to the faint; and to them that have no might he increaseth strength.

Isaiah 40:29

When you are weak, God enables you, reviving you when you faint and strengthening you when you fall. This can be true with your health, but it is always true with your spirit. Lean on God and be strong.

*And the people said unto Joshua,
The Lord our God will we serve,
and his voice will we obey.*

Joshua 24:24

Lord, I'm grateful today that you speak to us. By your Spirit, through your word, you give us direction and comfort. I will gladly serve you today, and listen to your voice.

My heart is toward the governors of Israel, that offered themselves willingly among the people. Bless ye the Lord.

Judges 5:9

I pray for governors and other officials today, grateful for their service on my behalf. Give them wisdom, Lord. Give them willing hearts to know and do your will.

Wherefore do ye spend money for that which is not bread? and your labour for that which satisfieth not? hearken diligently unto me, and eat ye that which is good, and let your soul delight itself in fatness.

Isaiah 55:2

We can invest a lot of time and energy in things that do not satisfy. But God invites us to his table, where the body and blood of his own Son meet our deepest need. Come and dine.

For I have satiated the weary soul, and I have replenished every sorrowful soul.

Jeremiah 31:25

Satiated is a great word—completely, I-can-not-eat-another-bite full of God's grace and blessing. Let him replenish your sorrowing soul today, and be filled with the goodness of God.

I will feed my flock, and I will cause them to lie down, saith the Lord God.

Ezekiel 34:15

Do you ever take a nap after a great meal? God's blessings are like that, filling and refreshing you in every way. Fill up and lie down today, content with the gracious blessings of God.

He answered and said, Lo, I see four men loose, walking in the midst of the fire, and they have no hurt; and the form of the fourth is like the Son of God.

Daniel 3:25

You are not alone in the fire. Likely you have three friends, but certainly you have one. The Son of God himself stands beside you, and you will suffer no hurt. He is faithful and you are loved.

He hath shewed thee, O man, what is good; and what doth the Lord require of thee, but to do justly, and to love mercy, and to walk humbly with thy God?

Micah 6:8

God's blessing includes a sense of what is necessary and good. Your conscience reminds you of what God requires—justice, and mercy, and humility. You know what you have to do. Do that and be blessed.

The Lord God is my strength, and he will make my feet like hinds' feet, and he will make me to walk upon mine high places.

Habakkuk 3:19

Lord, lift me up and let me stand in high places, able to see what is necessary and good. Give me certainty and give me strength, so I can know and do your will. And thank you, in advance.

The Lord hath taken away thy judgments, he hath cast out thine enemy: the king of Israel, even the Lord, is in the midst of thee: thou shalt not see evil any more.

Zephaniah 3:15

In Christ, the Lord has taken away your punishment and cast out your enemy, Satan. The king himself is with you; you are safe, and blessed, and loved. You are blessed indeed.

For where two or three are gathered together in my name, there am I in the midst of them.

Matthew 18:20

Your church is the place where two or three gather together in Christ's name. Go there often, for he is there, waiting to hear you and answer you. It is the fellowship of faith and a blessing from God.

And thou shalt love the Lord thy God with all thy heart, and with all thy soul, and with all thy mind, and with all thy strength: this is the first commandment.

Mark 12:30

Help me to do this, Lord, to love you with all my heart. There are many distractions and temptations, but this is the first commandment. With all my soul, mind, and strength I want to love you. Help me, Lord.

Be ye therefore merciful, as your Father also is merciful.

Luke 6:36

Your mercy is a blessing and comfort. Help me be merciful to others. Help me notice someone on the margins today, and help me speak to them with kindness and respect. This is your will, and I will do it.

If ye abide in me, and my words abide in you, ye shall ask what ye will, and it shall be done unto you.

John 15:7

It's easy to ask. It is not as easy to abide. There are so many distractions, not the least of which is your cell phone. Clear your mind, focus on Christ, and ask what you will. It will be a good day.

Thou hast made known to me the ways of life; thou shalt make me full of joy with thy countenance.

Acts 2:28

Lord, you have shown me the way of life. Help me to walk in it, filled with joyful obedience. I can see your face light up like a proud Father when I take my first steps. Bless me with joy.

What shall we then say to these things? If God be for us, who can be against us?

Romans 8:31

God is standing in your corner today, alert and available, ready to hold you up and even fight for you. Your life is safely his and all you can say is thanks.

But thanks be to God, which giveth us the victory through our Lord Jesus Christ.

1 Corinthians 15:57

The victory of which Paul speaks to the Corinthians is victory over death, the expectation of resurrection from the dead secured by Christ on Easter morning. No other blessing compares to this. Give thanks.

For God hath not given us the spirit of fear; but of power, and of love, and of a sound mind.

2 Timothy 1:7

Bless me Lord and conquer my fear. Fill me with hope, clearing my mind and giving me strength. With these blessings I can love as you love, fearlessly and fully. I will be blessed, and so will everyone I meet.

Opposites don’t attract nearly as often as they repel, if we are to believe the headlines. Pick a race, color, creed, or lifestyle, Lord of all, and we’ll find something to fight about. Deliver us from stereotypes. Inspire us to spot value in everyone we meet. As we dodge the curses and hatred, we are relieved there is room for all of us beneath your wings. Bless our diversity; may it flourish.

He is the Rock, his work is perfect: for all his ways are judgment: a God of truth and without iniquity, just and right is he.

Deuteronomy 32:4

His work is perfect. Think about that today when you doubt his plan or begin to complain. He is just and right. On this rock we stand; his truth will not shake or falter. Stand fast and behold his glory.

God, hear my prayer. Bless me with patience and a steadfast heart to help me get through such emotionally trying times. Heal the wounds of my heart and soul with the soothing balm of your comforting presence, that I may be able to love and to live again. Amen.

Then Samuel took a stone, and set it between Mizpeh and Shen, and called the name of it Ebenezer, saying, Hitherto hath the Lord helped us.

1 Samuel 7:12

Samuel set up a stone as a reminder of God's help. Flip through some photos today, remembering ways God has protected you or provided for you and those you love. Thus far, the Lord has helped you.

Then went king David in, and sat before the Lord, and he said, Who am I, O Lord God? and what is my house, that thou hast brought me hitherto?

2 Samuel 7:18

God promises David a descendant to build the temple (Solomon) and rule forever (Jesus). Even though you may not get to see or do some great work, God keeps his promises. For this, we are glad.

And he said, Lord God of Israel, there is no God like thee, in heaven above, or on earth beneath, who keepest covenant and mercy with thy servants that walk before thee with all their heart.

1 Kings 8:23

I'm grateful today, Lord, that there is no God like you, in heaven or in earth. You keep your promises and extend your mercy to those who walk before you. Give me strength and joy today.

Give unto the Lord the glory due unto his name: bring an offering, and come before him: worship the Lord in the beauty of holiness.

1 Chronicles 16:29

The only offering I bring today, Lord, is the sacrifice of praise. Reveal your glory and I will respond to your beauty, awed by your holiness, and grateful for your mercy.

And Hezekiah prayed before the Lord, and said, O Lord God of Israel, which dwellest between the cherubims, thou art the God, even thou alone, of all the kingdoms of the earth; thou hast made heaven and earth.

2 Kings 19:15

I delight in all you have made, Lord. And I delight in your reign over me and all the kingdoms of the world. You dwell in the heavens and concern yourself with the details of my days. Thank you, Lord.

Blessed be the Lord God of our fathers, which hath put such a thing as this in the king's heart, to beautify the house of the Lord which is in Jerusalem.

Ezra 7:27

As you face problems at work, remember God is able to put an idea in the heart of those you serve. In this way, he will make your life more beautiful and glorify his own name in your heart.

God is in the midst of her; she shall not be moved: God shall help her, and that right early.

Psalm 46:5

Her, here, is the people of God, worshipping in the Temple or the church on the corner. Wherever they gather, he is in the middle, her foundation and her help. When you gather with believers this week, you are blessed by him.

Lord,

In times of weakness and doubt, help us remember that you are always capable of miracles. Keep us ever alert to the possibility of visits from your ministering angels whom you send to protect and guide us.

May we receive them with a joyous and grateful heart and then pass on the blessings to others who need their comfort.

Amen

And said, O Lord God of our fathers, art not thou God in heaven? and rulest not thou over all the kingdoms of the heathen? and in thine hand is there not power and might, so that none is able to withstand thee?

2 Chronicles 20:6

Confronted with a coalition of armies, Jehoshaphat begins his prayer with gratitude for God's power. Whoever you face today, your God also rules, even over those who do not profess or follow him. Trust his power and might.

No matter where I travel
Or how far away I roam,
The greatest blessings that I have
Are found right here at home.

And said, I beseech thee, O Lord God of heaven, the great and terrible God, that keepeth covenant and mercy for them that love him and observe his commandments.

Nehemiah 1:5

If you are going to beg, beg God. He is the great and awesome promise keeper who has mercy on sinners. Like you. Come before him today, desperately and frequently. He alone can save.

But let all those that put their trust in thee rejoice: let them ever shout for joy, because thou defendest them: let them also that love thy name be joyful in thee.

Psalm 5:11

You protect me, Lord. Fill my heart with grateful joy. I want to shout your praise from the rooftop, or at least on social media. I love you, Lord. Give me your joy so everyone will know.

Wherefore David blessed the Lord before all the congregation: and David said, Blessed be thou, Lord God of Israel our father, for ever and ever.

1 Chronicles 29:10

It's one thing to praise God in the morning alone, over a cup of tea or coffee. But you must also praise him before the congregation. Private praise is good. Public praise is also good.

Thou, even thou, art Lord alone; thou hast made heaven, the heaven of heavens, with all their host, the earth, and all things that are therein, the seas, and all that is therein, and thou preservest them all; and the host of heaven worshippeth thee.

Nehemiah 9:6

Lord, you are Lord alone. You made me and everything around me. You preserve man and beast. Even the angels worship you. Show me your glory today, and fill my heart with grateful praise.

I would seek unto God, and unto God would I commit my cause: Which doeth great things and unsearchable; marvellous things without number.

Job 5:8–9

Lord, you do countless great, mysterious, and marvelous things. To you I commit my cause. As I seek your presence and your wisdom, Lord, fight for me. I need another great thing today.

I will be glad and rejoice in thee: I will sing praise to thy name, O thou most High.

Psalm 9:2

Your God is most high. The highest, the angels said at Christ's birth. Be like the angels. Sing his praise. Proclaim his glory. Be glad and rejoice in him.

Honour the Lord with thy substance, and with the firstfruits of all thine increase.

Proverbs 3:9

Help me be more generous today, Lord. I want to give more energy and resources to your work and to your children. Fill me with gratitude that overflows into the world around me.

The heavens declare the glory of God; and the firmament sheweth his handywork.

Psalm 19:1

Take some time tonight to contemplate the stars. Revel in the sunshine this morning, or even the rain. You will feel small, and God will seem big, as he should. Praise him.

Wisdom is the principal thing; therefore get wisdom: and with all thy getting get understanding.

Proverbs 4:7

When Solomon, already filled with wisdom, was asked what he wanted, he asked for more. He had great responsibility and opportunity. So do you. Ask for more wisdom to manage well.

Who is this King of glory? The Lord of hosts, he is the King of glory. Selah.

Psalm 24:10

Who is the king of glory? Sometimes we have to remind ourselves of these truths: our gracious king is glorious, above our capacity to imagine. And he is king, sovereign and righteous. Bow before the Lord of hosts.

O Lord, thou art my God; I will exalt thee, I will praise thy name; for thou hast done wonderful things; thy counsels of old are faithfulness and truth.

Isaiah 25:1

Embrace the counsels of old. The faithful and true testimony of God's word is as close as the Bible on your nightstand or the Bible app on your phone. Read it and be grateful.

He loveth righteousness and judgment: the earth is full of the goodness of the Lord.

Psalm 33:5

Consider how the Lord's goodness includes his righteous judgment. His law forbids us from hurting each other, and from hurting ourselves. What a mess life is, and how much messier it would be without his gracious law.

An altar of earth thou shalt make unto me, and shalt sacrifice thereon thy burnt offerings, and thy peace offerings, thy sheep, and thine oxen: in all places where I record my name I will come unto thee, and I will bless thee.

Exodus 20:24

Today you can come before God and praise him, no sacrifice required other than a grateful heart. He provided the necessary sacrifice, as a gift through his Son. Rejoice in this.

Remember that thou magnify his work, which men behold.

Job 36:24

Help me magnify your work, Lord, careful to seek your guidance and praise your name. May others see my gratitude and join my praise. Do your work in the world, Lord, and I will give you the credit.

Blessed be the Lord God of Israel from everlasting, and to everlasting. Amen, and Amen.

Psalm 41:13

A double Amen for the Lord's eternal loving kindness! Long before you were born and forever past your last breath, he is the same and he is good, caring for his children. Forever.

For I know that my redeemer liveth, and that he shall stand at the latter day upon the earth.

Job 19:25

For this I am glad, dear Jesus, that you are alive, and you will return. Root me in this reality, giving me hope and gratitude each moment of my days. Fill my mouth with praise.

Great is the Lord, and greatly to be praised in the city of our God, in the mountain of his holiness.

Psalm 48:1

Lord may my gratitude for you reach new heights today. Bring me into the mountain of your holiness, far above yet fully present in my current circumstance. Great are you, Lord.

Sing, O ye heavens; for the Lord hath done it: shout, ye lower parts of the earth: break forth into singing, ye mountains, O forest, and every tree therein: for the Lord hath redeemed Jacob, and glorified himself in Israel.

Isaiah 44:23

Time to shout and sing, for the Lord has redeemed you and glorified himself. Regardless of your highs and lows, he is drawing you to himself with love and mercy. Be demonstratively glad!

Make a joyful noise unto God, all ye lands.

Psalm 66:1

I can make a joyful noise today, Lord. Make me aware of others, both nearby and far away, who praise you. Let me hear the singing in distant lands and in the desk next to mine. All the lands will praise you.

We will not hide them from their children, shewing to the generation to come the praises of the Lord, and his strength, and his wonderful works that he hath done.

Psalm 78:4

Help me, merciful Father, to show the next generation reasons to praise you. You are strong and do wonderful works. Give me a chance to show my gratitude with my children and grandchildren and to the kids next door.

I am the Lord, and there is none else, there is no God beside me: I girded thee, though thou hast not known me.

Isaiah 45:5

Even when you were unaware, God was giving you the strength you needed to know and do his will. There is no God beside him. But he is beside you. For this, be glad.

The Lord reigneth, he is clothed with majesty; the Lord is clothed with strength, wherewith he hath girded himself: the world also is stablished, that it cannot be moved.

Psalm 93:1

I'm grateful, Father, that the world cannot be moved. By your strength and might, there is stability and order in creation. Make it so in my life as well, and I will praise you.

The stars come nightly to the sky;
The tidal wave unto the sea;
Nor time, nor space, nor deep, nor high
Can keep my own away from me.
Friendship is the triple alliance
of the three great
powers, Love, Sympathy, and Help.
My friends have come to me
unsought; the great
God gave them to me.
—Ralph Waldo Emerson

O worship the Lord in the beauty of holiness: fear before him, all the earth.

Psalm 96:9

Oh, Lord, your harmony, purity, and transcendence inspire awe in my heart. All these are beautifully expressed at the cross, where your holiness and love meet. Fill me with gratitude today.

Ah Lord God! behold, thou hast made the heaven and the earth by thy great power and stretched out arm, and there is nothing too hard for thee.

Jeremiah 32:17

This great truth has encouraged believers since Adam and Eve–there is nothing too hard for God. Your creator and redeemer is stretching out his arm to you and around you. Rejoice!

To appoint unto them that mourn in Zion, to give unto them beauty for ashes, the oil of joy for mourning, the garment of praise for the spirit of heaviness.

Isaiah 61:3

What loss do you mourn? A loved one or old friend? An opportunity or pleasure? God can replace the spirit of heaviness with a garment of praise, turning ashes into beauty. Let him come to you with the oil of joy.

Bless the Lord, O my soul. O Lord my God, thou art very great; thou art clothed with honour and majesty.

Psalm 104:1

You are clothed with honor and majesty, Lord. You are, as the Psalmist says, very great. I'm humbled in your presence and grateful for your love. From so far above it reaches down to me, filling me with joy.

Call unto me, and I will answer thee, and shew thee great and mighty things, which thou knowest not.

Jeremiah 33:3

You may not know exactly what you are praying for, but God knows exactly what you need. He will show you great and mighty things. Just call and he will answer.

Now I Nebuchadnezzar praise and extol and honour the King of heaven, all whose works are truth, and his ways judgment: and those that walk in pride he is able to abase.

Daniel 4:37

In view of God's judgment, even this pagan king began to extol and honor Daniel's God. Someday every knee will bow, and every tongue confess the greatness of our God. Be grateful that you can start today.

Thank you, God, for letting me survive this tragedy. I am glad that I have been given another chance in this world. Although it will be hard to start over, I realize that this is an opportunity for me to decide the importance of things. Please comfort me as I consider this. Amen.

It is he that buildeth his stories in the heaven, and hath founded his troop in the earth; he that calleth for the waters of the sea, and poureth them out upon the face of the earth: The Lord is his name.

Amos 9:6

You may be aware of many things God has done for you. But contemplate the many things he is doing around you. The sky, the sea, the unseen angels: these are all his work. And this great God cares about you.

The glory of this latter house shall be greater than of the former, saith the Lord of hosts: and in this place will I give peace, saith the Lord of hosts.

Haggai 2:9

After the exile, those who had seen Solomon's magnificent temple were disheartened by the modest new one. But the prophet says its glory will be greater, because Jesus will come there. And he has come, to the temple and to you.

Then he answered and spake unto me, saying, This is the word of the Lord unto Zerubbabel, saying, Not by might, nor by power, but by my spirit, saith the Lord of hosts.

Zechariah 4:6

A little overwhelmed and surrounded by enemies, Zerubbabel is reminded that the reconstruction of the temple depends not on human strength but on the Spirit of God working in and through his people. Take heart. It is still true.

One thing have I desired of the Lord, that will I seek after; that I may dwell in the house of the Lord all the days of my life, to behold the beauty of the Lord, and to enquire in his temple.

Psalm 27:4

It is great to be in your house, Lord, gathering with other believers to praise and worship you. When we desire you, and seek you, we hear from you. It is a small taste of heaven's joy.

And one cried unto another, and said, Holy, holy, holy, is the Lord of hosts: the whole earth is full of his glory.

Isaiah 6:3

This is the song of angels, the three-fold holiness of God on a throne. This is why the earth is full of his glory, people like you praising him as the angels do. Give voice to your praise and join the chorus.

But Jesus beheld them, and said unto them, With men this is impossible; but with God all things are possible.

Matthew 19:26

Jesus asks a rich young ruler to give up everything and follow him. The young man walks away, sorrowful. Then Jesus says such service and sacrifice is possible, but only with God's help. For what sacrifice or service do you need his help today?

Behold, God is my salvation; I will trust, and not be afraid: for the Lord Jehovah is my strength and my song; he also is become my salvation.

Isaiah 12:2

In a short song of praise, Isaiah refers to God as Lord Jehovah. Lord reflects his eternal, self-existent nature. Jehovah reinforces his covenant-keeping character. For this we are most grateful: our eternal God keeps his promises.

We are blessed by your enveloping spirit as near to us as daily changing weather. Your comfort touches us like gentle rain and hushed snow. And, like the sound of thunder and glimpse of searing lightning, you startle us with new opportunities.

For he that is mighty hath done to me great things; and holy is his name.

Luke 1:49

Make a list of the great things God has done to you, not for you. We are seldom grateful for the ways he is changing us. But that is the goal. What has he taught you? How are you different?

And let the peace of God rule in your hearts, to the which also ye are called in one body; and be ye thankful.

Colossians 3:15

Considering all the blessings we could count, we are quick to include God's peace—the promise of the angels on Christmas day. But the unity we have with other believers is also on God's list. Make sure it is on yours.

Praising God, and having favour with all the people. And the Lord added to the church daily such as should be saved.

Acts 2:47

People were drawn to the early church because they were positive and hopeful, praising God day and night. What can churches today learn from their example? Start by cultivation your own grateful heart.

We recognize your angelic messengers in the welcoming support and open-handed suggestions of others willing to share how we, too, can learn to live in the new ways that illness or trouble sometimes dictates. We see your hand in the clever, creative, and determined adaptations they pass on to us and are carried as if by a thousand lifting wings.

And I prayed unto the Lord my God, and made my confession, and said, O Lord, the great and dreadful God, keeping the covenant and mercy to them that love him, and to them that keep his commandments.

Daniel 9:4

Daniel praises God's attributes, a key element of prayer. And he confesses his own sin, also an important part of our prayer. If you love God, come before him and do both.

The name of the Lord is a strong tower: the righteous runneth into it, and is safe.

Proverbs 18:10

If you need a tower, you want a strong one. You can go there and be safe. God is such a tower, an enduring refuge in the battle for your soul. Be grateful for his protection and run to him.

And we know that all things work together for good to them that love God, to them who are the called according to his purpose.

Romans 8:28

Are you grateful to be called according to his purpose? If you love him, he is orchestrating all things for your good and his plan. For this promise, be glad today.

But by the grace of God I am what I am: and his grace which was bestowed upon me was not in vain; but I laboured more abundantly than they all: yet not I, but the grace of God which was with me.

1 Corinthians 15:10

You are who you are, by the grace of God. Has his grace been given in vain? Or do you work harder and gratefully because of his grace, without comparing it to others? His grace is with you today. It is enough.

I am crucified with Christ: nevertheless I live; yet not I, but Christ liveth in me: and the life which I now live in the flesh I live by the faith of the Son of God, who loved me, and gave himself for me.

Galatians 2:20

Lord, crucify my selfish desire and willful pride today. Live in me, as with your strength I love and give myself for others, as you did. I am grateful for the life you gave me and for the resurrection to come.

When life goes awry, Lord, I need someone to blame so I point the finger at you. Heaven help me, I want it both ways: you as sender and fixer of trouble. Help me know you don't will trouble, for what could you possibly gain? And when the good you want for me isn't possible in the randomness of life, I know you are with me.

And when he had consulted with the people, he appointed singers unto the Lord, and that should praise the beauty of holiness.

2 Chronicles 20:21

As king, David had a lot to do, but not so much he could not make sure that God was praised. What's on your schedule today? Between the errands and obligations, make sure to contemplate the majesty and beauty of God. And praise him.

I can do all things through Christ which strengtheneth me.

Philippians 4:13

In this verse, the thing the Apostle can do with God’s strength is to be content. God doesn’t give us superhuman ability: he gives us confidence in his plan and provision. To be content, we need his help.

Giving thanks unto the Father, which hath made us meet to be partakers of the inheritance of the saints in light.

Colossians 1:12

The inheritance of the saints in light is a common hope shared by all who belong to God's family: to stand in the presence of God. His truth, holiness, and purity are our great and confident expectation.

Blessed be the God and Father of our Lord Jesus Christ, which according to his abundant mercy hath begotten us again unto a lively hope by the resurrection of Jesus Christ from the dead.

1 Peter 1:3

Give me a lively hope, Father, a fresh joy in all you are and all you provide. You raised Jesus from the dead, and you can refresh my dull and aching spirit with hope and strength. Please, Lord. And thanks.

Pay cuts and wage freezes have come as a shock, Lord, and I'm working harder for less. Help me learn to balance not just the checkbook but my consumer appetites as well, so I can decide what's really important, in both lean and fat times. And help me to remember all you have already given me.

Rejoice evermore.

1 Thessalonians 5:16

Paul ends his first letter to the church in Thessalonica with a series of short instructions. And this is one: express gratitude rooted in your relationship with God and the hope of eternal life, not fleeting emotions or external situations.

And I thank Christ Jesus our Lord, who hath enabled me, for that he counted me faithful, putting me into the ministry.

1 Timothy 1:12

Paul had started out persecuting the early church and ended up as an Apostle of God's grace. Be grateful that God has changed you, and enabled you to testify of him.

Let us therefore come boldly unto the throne of grace, that we may obtain mercy, and find grace to help in time of need.

Hebrews 4:16

I am so needy, Lord. Today I feel weak and unworthy, but through your Son I can come boldly before your throne and find mercy and grace. In your Son's name I come, with confidence and hope.

Thou art worthy, O Lord, to receive glory and honour and power: for thou hast created all things, and for thy pleasure they are and were created.

Revelation 4:11

I am not capable of fully expressing my gratitude, Lord, for you are worthy of honor and glory I cannot comprehend. But it gives you pleasure when I try. So, accept my humble sacrifice of praise.

I will praise the Lord according to his righteousness: and will sing praise to the name of the Lord most high.

Psalm 7:17

To praise God according to his righteousness is to praise him a lot, for he is altogether righteous. He defines it, as he is the source of every good act or word. Sing praise to the most high.

Thou therefore, my son, be strong in the grace that is in Christ Jesus.

2 Timothy 2:1

Help me be strong, Father, as a grateful child fully aware of your incomparable grace. You have saved me, blessed me, and changed me. I am strengthened by this. And I am glad.

Thank you, loving God, for my mother with whom I share a deep connection. For it was her loving care and ceaseless attention that has empowered me. I am humbled by her steadfastness and am much blessed.

And every creature which is in heaven, and on the earth, and under the earth, and such as are in the sea, and all that are in them, heard I saying, Blessing, and honour, and glory, and power, be unto him that sitteth upon the throne, and unto the Lamb for ever and ever.

Revelation 5:13

A scroll is brought forth in heaven and no one can open it. Then Jesus steps forth, not as a lion but as a lamb, slain for sin. He opens the scroll of God's plan. And we can and should praise him, as heaven did.

When trouble strikes, we're restored by the smallest gestures from God's ambassadors: friends, random kindnesses, shared pain and support, even a stranger's outstretched hand. And we get the message: God cares.

Her children arise up, and call her blessed; her husband also, and he praiseth her.

Proverbs 31:28

This morning was a fiasco. My husband needed to catch an early train, my son couldn't find a textbook, and our dog scarfed down the bread I'd intended for everyone's lunch sandwiches. I was feeling pretty frazzled, and had to get to work myself. But after the boys got out the door and I'd made sure the dog was none the worse for wear, I took a deep breath and noticed that Ben had made me a pot of coffee. My husband had promised he'd order us a pizza tonight so that no one had to cook. And our dog? Well, it's hard to stay mad at a smiling dog! Lord, even when things are a little crazy around our house, I thank you: I am blessed by my family.

Charity suffereth long, and is kind; charity envieth not; charity vaunteth not itself, is not puffed up.

1 Corinthians 13:4

Countless books and movies have been dedicated to love. In many stories, love is romantic, heedless and "I"-based. Am I the object of affection? Yet God teaches us that love (referred to as charity in the King James Version of the Bible) is a two-way exchange of something much more profound: its very nature is selfless and humble. Love isn't, in fact, the flash and show; it's a grounded exchange, a deep, mutual caring and respect that endures long after the first brilliant connection. When we know true love, we feel no need to flaunt it.

For, brethren, ye have been called unto liberty; only use not liberty for an occasion to the flesh, but by love serve one another. For all the law is fulfilled in one word, even in this; Thou shalt love thy neighbour as thyself.

Galatians 5:13–14

I am grateful to live in a society where I can live freely and do as I please. I have a steady job, which consequently allows me to pursue interests that include travel and food. I enjoy exploring new cuisines, for example, and cooking for and eating out with friends. I feel lucky to be free to engage in these experiences, yet I also know that reaching out to others is an important part of becoming a fulfilled, evolved person. To that end, I volunteered with Meals on Wheels. I have already met some cool seniors. I find myself looking forward to socializing with them each week. God, help me to honor the freedom I enjoy by helping others, not just by indulging myself.

Yea, though I walk through the valley of the shadow of death, I will fear no evil: for thou art with me; thy rod and thy staff they comfort me.

Psalm 23:4

This past year has been a challenging one. My son flunked several of his first-semester classes and returned home. My husband and I are doing our best to support him emotionally, and we have talked, as a family, about Gary getting a job and earning some extra money while he regroups. But he is very depressed and finding it difficult to make decisions, and I myself am deeply saddened by his unhappiness. Dear Lord, your loving presence provides solace. Please comfort him. Please fill my heart, and help my husband and me to know how to encourage our son and help him work through this difficult chapter.

That in blessing I will bless thee, and in multiplying I will multiply thy seed as the stars of the heaven, and as the sand which is upon the sea shore; and thy seed shall possess the gate of his enemies.

Genesis 22:17

There are some things you can't count. The blessings of God are among them. He multiplies our impact and he multiplies our victories daily. He blesses us in our blessings, for which we are glad.

And all these blessings shall come on thee, and overtake thee, if thou shalt hearken unto the voice of the Lord thy God.

Deuteronomy 28:2

Not only do all God's blessings come, they come faster and faster, and get bigger and bigger. They overtake us. Please Lord, let me hear your voice today and recognize your goodness.

Blessed is the man that walketh not in the counsel of the ungodly, nor standeth in the way of sinners, nor sitteth in the seat of the scornful.

Psalm 1:1

It is a blessing to have good friends, friends who love you and love God, friends who don't make fun of you or give you bad advice. Make a list of such friends. And thank God for them.

Fear thou not; for I am with thee: be not dismayed; for I am thy God: I will strengthen thee; yea, I will help thee; yea, I will uphold thee with the right hand of my righteousness.

Isaiah 41:10

Consider all this: he is with you, he strengthens you, he helps you, and he upholds you. So why worry? He is your God and his hand comforts and protects you. Fear not and be not dismayed. He is with you. Always.

Let your light so shine before men, that they may see your good works, and glorify your Father which is in heaven.

Matthew 5:16

I am by nature a quiet person. When our pastor recently gave a sermon challenging us to go out and share with others the way God has helped us grow, I felt resistant. "Not my style!" was my reaction. But after the service, I realized that showing reverence to God could take different forms. I don't have to go out and preach about how God has helped me improve myself. I can simply demonstrate growth through my actions, whether I'm quitting smoking or getting better at managing my temper. If people ask, as someone recently did, "How did you quit smoking?" I can always give a simple answer: "Prayer." Lord, I can demonstrate my beliefs and inspire others by striving to better myself.

The Lord is my shepherd; I shall not want.

Psalm 23:1

What a blessing, a shepherd who leads you into green pastures beside still waters. You have a shepherd who feeds you, protects you, and loves you. He knows your name and walks beside you, even in the valley of death. What more could you want?

Lay not up for yourselves treasures upon earth, where moth and rust doth corrupt, and where thieves break through and steal: But lay up for yourselves treasures in heaven, where neither moth nor rust doth corrupt, and where thieves do not break through nor steal: For where your treasure is, there will your heart be also.

Matthew 6:19–21

When my wife and I were first married, we would spend weeks looking for just the right couch; even a dish drainer was chosen after deliberation. Then when our daughter was born, the "look" of the house was sometimes sacrificed for practicalities. As our daughter grew, we adopted two cats. That couch we chose with such care has taken quite a beating. With kids and pets running around, the house isn't quite the showplace we nurtured. But it's a happy home. Sometimes things break. Sometimes things get torn or stained. It doesn't seem to matter the way it once did. Thank you, God, for helping me to learn where my treasure truly lies.

Delight thyself also in the Lord; and he shall give thee the desires of thine heart.

Psalm 37:4

As our delights change, so do our desires. This means the more we know him the more we change, as the desires of our hearts become the desires of his. How can you delight in him today? How will it change what you want and what you do?

He that loveth silver shall not be satisfied with silver; nor he that loveth abundance with increase: this is also vanity.

Ecclesiastes 5:10

For a period of years, I enjoyed a high-powered job with a significant income. But looking back, I can see that I labored under the misconception that possessions would bring satisfaction. Unfortunately, that was not the case. Soon after I bought my home, I bought a second one. I spent a lot of time maintaining possessions and many days I felt dissatisfied. It was only when I made the decision to simplify my life, to divest myself of some of the possessions that were taking up so much of my time and focus instead on matters of substance, including my relationships with others and my own spirituality, that I gained some measure of peace. God, help me to stay focused on what matters.

But if any provide not for his own, and specially for those of his own house, he hath denied the faith, and is worse than an infidel.

1 Timothy 5:8

When my stepfather died, he left a sum of money to me. I was surprised and at first a little overwhelmed, but my wife and I consulted with a financial planner. We wanted to be wise stewards of this unexpected income. After our meeting, we determined that we would use a large portion of the money for our daughter's college education, and put aside the rest for retirement. Because of health concerns I've been facing, it is important to me to know that my wife will have money to draw upon in the likely event that I die before she does. God, wealth gives me an obligation to provide for my family. I am grateful for the means to do so.

Blessed be the Lord, who daily loadeth us with benefits, even the God of our salvation. Selah.

Psalm 68:19

The great thing about our daily bread is that you need it and receive it daily. And you receive it in overflowing abundance. Make a list. Be grateful. Sing a song or do a little dance. God provides all you need, even the salvation of your soul.

And when she had opened it, she saw the child: and, behold, the babe wept. And she had compassion on him, and said, This is one of the Hebrews' children.

Exodus 2:6

We have recently begun thinking about adoption. The thought of helping a parentless child is meaningful to us, and we've started investigating what it might mean to adopt a child from another culture. Our friends recently adopted a little girl, and their journey and the joy they've experienced fill us with hope. We know we have a lot of love to give. God, please guide us as we endeavor to reach out to a child in need. Please keep us humble and cognizant of how much we stand to gain by showing compassion to another.

Hearken unto thy father that begat thee, and despise not thy mother when she is old.

Proverbs 23:22

Throughout my life I have enjoyed many milestones: attaining a college degree, securing my first job, marriage, the birth of my children, and seeing my relationship with my parents flip as they age and begin to rely on me as I once relied on them. Each life chapter has brought its joys and trials, and while it is my privilege to support my mom and dad, I confess that their new vulnerability sometimes fills me with fear. My children, in high school now, still need me, perhaps more than ever as they face challenges of their own. Sometimes I feel as though there are not enough hours in the day to work and make sure the needs of my loved ones are met. God, as I grow older and my life becomes more complicated, please help me to remember to always honor my mother and father. May I never forget them or shirk my responsibilities amid the everyday cares of working and parenting.

Bless these children, God. Keep them growing in mind and body. Keep them ever moving and reaching out toward the objects of their curiosity. And may they find, in all their explorations, the one thing that holds it all together: your love.

The righteous shall flourish like the palm tree: he shall grow like a cedar in Lebanon. Those that be planted in the house of the Lord shall flourish in the courts of our God. They shall still bring forth fruit in old age; they shall be fat and flourishing.

Psalm 92:12–14

As a boy, I had a close relationship with my grandfather, who had a little house in northern Michigan. My parents and I would go see him every summer, and I'd take long walks with him. As I became a teen, though, I was drawn more and more to my friends. One summer I told my parents that I didn't want to go. I still remember my dad's response: "There will come a day when your grandpa is no longer with us. You will be glad of the times you shared when he is gone." I reluctantly agreed. It turned out that visit was an especially good one. My grandfather taught me how to play chess, and though he had started to walk with a cane, we still hiked the property. The following winter, a heart attack took his life. To this day, I feel tremendous gratitude that I shared that last special visit with a man whose decency continues to inspire me.

Then sang Moses and the children of Israel this song unto the Lord, and spake, saying, I will sing unto the Lord, for he hath triumphed gloriously: the horse and his rider hath he thrown into the sea.

Exodus 15:1

Do you feel like a tightly wound rubber band, about to snap as you juggle work and family and commitments? Remember, your God has triumphed gloriously. Be grateful for his strength, especially when you lack your own.

For I came down from heaven, not to do mine own will, but the will of him that sent me.

John 6:38

Even Jesus, speaking here, did not do his own will, but the will of the Father. In the mystery of the triune God, this is beyond our understanding. But it is not beyond our capability. We too can do the will of the Father. We can pray for it. We can desire it. If there was one way you could be like Jesus today, it would be this: do the will of the One who sent him. And don't worry about all the things you don't understand. Start with what you know. Do that.

Get wisdom, get understanding: forget it not; neither decline from the words of my mouth. Forsake her not, and she shall preserve thee: love her, and she shall keep thee. Wisdom is the principal thing; therefore get wisdom: and with all thy getting get understanding.

Proverbs 4:5–7

It's easy to get stuff. It's not easy to get wisdom. We have to want it, seek it, love it, and remember it. But the rewards are greater than any loyalty program offered online. The benefit is understanding. The reward is life itself, preserved and kept by a holy God, a God for whom our reverence and awe is the beginning of wisdom. This wisdom is the principal thing, a priceless treasure, and an eternal perspective.

He healeth the broken in heart,
and bindeth up their wounds.

Psalm 147:3

Lord, heal my heart. I have many scars, and they didn't come from sticks and stones. They came from careless words, unkind things people said to me, or that I said to myself. But you can heal me. You can remove the bitterness I feel and replace it with sweet spirit. You can replace my deep sadness with joy. You can flood the barrenness of my soul with springs of living water, washing and binding my wounds with your mercy. Please, Lord, do this. Amen.

The blessings of family:

Family is our foundation, our roots, and our source of identity.

Family loves us through the best times and the worst times.

Family gets us—our quirks, our jokes, our wit and wisdom.

Family always tells it to us straight.

Family means we are never alone in the world.

Family is where the heart is, and where we call home.

But as it is written, Eye hath not seen, nor ear heard, neither have entered into the heart of man, the things which God hath prepared for them that love him.

1 Corinthians 2:9

We can't even imagine all that God has prepared for us in heaven. Or even before we get there. As Saint Francis of Assisi said, "Praise be to you, my Lord, for all the blessings you have given and for those yet to come."

Rejoicing in hope; patient in tribulation; continuing instant in prayer.

Romans 12:12

Lord, help me to rejoice in hope and be patient in my trials. When I need patience or hope, help me turn to you instantly. Your constant and powerful presence is all I need today. You are all I need. And I am blessed.

Because he hath set his love upon me, therefore will I deliver him: I will set him on high, because he hath known my name. He shall call upon me, and I will answer him: I will be with him in trouble; I will deliver him, and honour him.

Psalm 91:14–15

There is a principle here, repeated often in scripture, that applies to all believers in all times: "He shall call upon me, and I will answer him." In any time of trouble, the Lord hears the cry of his people. In Psalm 50:15 he says, "Call upon me in the day of trouble: I will deliver thee, and thou shalt glorify me." It is God's own honor at stake. He wants to be known for helping his children. He is exalted when we turn to him.

And I will give you pastors according to mine heart, which shall feed you with knowledge and understanding.

Jeremiah 3:15

In the days of Josiah the king, Jeremiah calls Israel back to God. When they return God says, "I will give you pastors according to my heart." It has always been so. God sends leaders to his people: prophets, kings, priests, and pastors. The word pastor means shepherd, and the Apostle Peter counsels, "Feed the flock of God which is among you," not as lords but as examples (1 Peter 5:2–3). In this they imitate Christ, who called himself the good shepherd.

The Lord is gracious, and full of compassion; slow to anger, and of great mercy.

Psalm 145:8

This reflects God's mercy and is echoed other times in the Psalms. But it appears first in Exodus. Moses takes a second tablet up Mount Sinai to be inscribed with God's law. Moses had every reason to be anxious. He had broken the first tablet and the people had worshipped a golden calf. But the Lord describes himself to Moses as merciful and gracious and not a God like other gods. He is slow to anger and great in mercy. Moses "bowed his head toward the earth" (Exodus 34:8). And so should we.

And Jesus said unto them, I am the bread of life: he that cometh to me shall never hunger; and he that believeth on me shall never thirst.

John 6:35

The crowd has come for loaves and fishes. The miracle of Jesus feeding 5,000 is fresh on their minds. But Jesus says he has something better. He is himself the bread of life. If we come to him we will never hunger, he says. The crowd is startled and confused, even angry. What is he talking about? But Jesus insists: "He that believeth on me hath everlasting life . . . the bread that I will give is my flesh, which I will give for the life of the world." (verses 47–51). His promise is that he can fill us, nurture us, and satisfy us. With food like this we can live forever.

My God hath sent his angel, and hath shut the lions' mouths, that they have not hurt me: forasmuch as before him innocency was found in me; and also before thee, O king, have I done no hurt.

Daniel 6:22

Not every promise in the Bible is explicit. Daniel tells the king that God had protected him from the lions although there is nothing to suggest this was promised specifically. Daniel had seen God protect the three Hebrew children in the furnace (Daniel 3), and he knew God would send angels to protect him.

Angels fed the prophet Elijah and often carried out the work of God in the world. Jesus himself said that children have angels who see the face of God in heaven (Matthew 18:10). As Jerome, one of the church fathers, puts it, "how great the dignity of the soul, since each one has from his birth an angel commissioned to guard it."

My head with oil thou didst not anoint: but this woman hath anointed my feet with ointment. Wherefore I say unto thee, Her sins, which are many, are forgiven; for she loved much: but to whom little is forgiven, the same loveth little.

Luke 7:46–47

Let me be as extravagant in my love for you, Jesus, as the woman who anointed your feet with oil. Let me freely admit my sins, and my debt to you, so that I may be forgiven.

By faith Moses, when he was born, was hid three months of his parents, because they saw he was a proper child; and they were not afraid of the king's commandment.

Hebrews 11:23

My husband and I have three children under the age of ten. We love being parents, even as we understand that parenting can entail sacrifice. This came home to us recently when my husband declined an opportunity for promotion. Though the job sounded interesting, it meant that he would be traveling three weeks out of every four. We have decided our priority, right now, is for both of us to hold jobs where we can be consistently home and together as a family. The job offer was good, but the timing was not. Though these decisions can be difficult, God reminds us to sacrifice happily for our children. If we sometimes have to defer our own gratification, seeing our children thrive is a blessing.

Blessed are the poor in spirit: for theirs is the kingdom of heaven.

Matthew 5:3

What's the most important thing you have to do today? Approach it with humility, inviting God's blessings and asking for his strength. While he resists the proud, he gives special grace to those who are poor of spirit. Theirs is the kingdom.

Father God, we know that to receive the blessing of healing, the heart must be open. But when we are mad, we close off the heart as if it were a prison. Remind us that a heart that is shut cannot receive understanding, acceptance, and renewal. Even though we feel angry, we must keep the heart's door slightly ajar so your grace can enter and fill our darkness with the light of hope.

But the salvation of the righteous is of the Lord: he is their strength in the time of trouble.

Psalm 37:39

Every time has its own trouble, every day its own challenges. But the Lord provides strength and salvation. Sometimes we need both. Thankfully there is a limitless supply. When we get that unexpected phone call or run into that difficult person, the Lord can help us make the right decision or respond in the right way. He is our strength in time of trouble.

I will bless the Lord, who hath given me counsel: my reins also instruct me in the night seasons.

Psalm 16:7

Dear God, I need your wisdom today. I have a difficult decision to make or an awkward conversation to have. Show me what to do or what to say. Instruct me, and I will be grateful.

And this is the will of him that sent me, that every one which seeth the Son, and believeth on him, may have everlasting life: and I will raise him up at the last day.

John 6:40

The promise here is not that everyone will have everlasting life, but that everyone who sees the Son and believes on him will. More than that, God will raise them up at the end of time. Just look at the Son and believe. This is the very will of God. How do we see him? By faith. Just look and believe. The rest is up to a God who keeps his promises.

From the dark night of the soul
Comes the blessing of the dawn.
From the deep wounds of the heart
Comes the gift of love reborn.
From the chaos of confusion
Comes the calm of clarity.
From the anguish of discord
Comes the peace of harmony.
From the grieving of great loss
Comes the happiness of new life.
From the coldness of despair
Comes the warmth of our Father's light.

Blessed is the man that trusteth in the Lord, and whose hope the Lord is.

Jeremiah 17:7

Biblical hope leads to confident expectation, not wishful thinking. It is rooted in the character and purpose of God. We trust the Lord, because he is faithful and true. Let your confidence be in the eternal, unchanging nature of God. Have hope and be blessed.

Blessed are they that mourn: for they shall be comforted.

Matthew 5:4

It's hard to see mourning as a blessing, but that is to mistake the thing we mourn for the comfort we receive. The reassuring comfort of God is the blessing we need, especially in moments of grief and loss. In those moments, he is tender and gracious.

Bless our differences, O Lord. And let us love across all barriers, the walls we build of color, culture, and language. Let us turn our eyes upward and remember: The God who made us all lives and breathes and moves within us, untouched by our petty distinctions. Let us love him as he is, for he loves us just as we are.

And there came a leper to him, beseeching him, and kneeling down to him, and saying unto him, If thou wilt, thou canst make me clean. And Jesus, moved with compassion, put forth his hand, and touched him, and saith unto him, I will; be thou clean.

Mark 1:40–41

There is no problem too big for God to help us with it, no wound or hurt too deep for healing. Cleanse us, Lord, of all that hurts us and hinders us emotionally, spiritually, and physically.

His lord said unto him, Well done, thou good and faithful servant: thou hast been faithful over a few things, I will make thee ruler over many things: enter thou into the joy of thy lord.

Matthew 25:21

Lord, when I get to the end of my life, I really want to hear you say "well done." So, help me to be faithful today, in the many and little things you set before me. Give me a glimpse of the joy before me. Give me wisdom and strength.

Father, you will help us to survive the seasons of surprises in our lives. For just as the harshest winter always gives way to the warm blush of spring, the season of our suffering will give way to a brighter tomorrow, where change becomes a catalyst for new growth and spiritual maturity. Amen.

For God so loved the world, that he gave his only begotten Son, that whosoever believeth in him should not perish, but have everlasting life.

John 3:16

There is a reason this verse is so familiar. It is repeated often because it clearly states all we need to know. God loved us. He gave his Son for us. All we have to do is believe. It's a simple truth that changes everything. Even the life to come.

And let the peace of God rule in your hearts, to the which also ye are called in one body; and be ye thankful.

Colossians 3:15

When we focus on ourselves we sometimes fail to appreciate the blessing of being called in one body, the church. Let others encourage you today; it's one way the peace of God will rule in your heart.

In every thing give thanks: for this is the will of God in Christ Jesus concerning you.

1 Thessalonians 5:18

"Help me, O God, to see your blessings in every trial and to praise you in all things."

—Susanna Wesley, mother of 19 children including John and Charles

Heavenly Father, I ask for your healing presence as I try to remember the good things in my life. Protect me from the worldly hurts and evil that have clouded my life and robbed me of joy. Help me forget the past, to let go of grudges, and to make a new start. Take away the darkness of my sorrow, and flood it with the light of your love. Forgive me, so I might forgive others. Amen.

Saying, Surely blessing I will bless thee, and multiplying I will multiply thee.

Hebrews 6:14

This was one of God's many promises to Abraham. And it's true for you, too. You can never completely count your blessings, although it is good to try. Our God blesses us and continues to bless us, without number and over generations. Be encouraged by this.

Saying, Amen: Blessing, and glory, and wisdom, and thanksgiving, and honour, and power, and might, be unto our God for ever and ever. Amen.

Revelation 7:12

Revelation is a book about end times and last things. It is good to remember that in the end this is all that's left: praise to our God for who he is. Amen!

Sing the wondrous love of Jesus,
Sing his mercy and his grace;
In the mansions bright and blessed,
He'll prepare for us a place.
While we walk the pilgrim pathway,
Clouds will overspread the sky;
But when trav'ling days are over,
Not a shadow, not a sigh.
When we all get to heaven,
What a day of rejoicing that will be!
When we all see Jesus,
We'll sing and shout the victory.

—Eliza E. Hewitt, "When
We All Get To Heaven"

If any of you lack wisdom, let him ask of God, that giveth to all men liberally, and upbraideth not; and it shall be given him.

James 1:5

I pray for wisdom and understanding for my fellow humans. So often my family, friends, and colleagues get on my nerves and create drama. I find myself wanting to turn away. I know they are as human and flawed as I am, but my patience is short. Please help me to look beyond their behaviors to the sweet and wonderful souls they are inside, and to understand where their own fears and frustrations are coming from. Rarely is it even personal, so help me to stop taking it all so personally and just be there for them on good days and on bad, as a true friend would, without judgment.

Lord, we confess that our thoughts and beliefs can act as our outstretched wings or prison bars. Save us from the downward spiral where we think defeating thoughts, become depressed, and then act in hopeless ways. Break the cycle, O Lord! Set us free from ideas that imprison our minds and shackle our actions. Restore us to balance so we may soar through the peaks and the valleys with outstretched wings. Amen.

If he offer it for a thanksgiving, then he shall offer with the sacrifice of thanksgiving unleavened cakes mingled with oil, and unleavened wafers anointed with oil, and cakes mingled with oil, of fine flour, fried.

Leviticus 7:12

This verse provides instructions for the peace offerings, voluntary sacrifices to express gratitude, fulfillment of vows, or devotion. Whatever sacrifice we offer, however, must be accompanied by actual thanksgiving. God wants our heart most of all.

That I may publish with the voice of thanksgiving, and tell of all thy wondrous works.

Psalm 26:7

Your great mercy, Lord, is on my lips. I want to tell my children and my friends about your kindness, delighting in your works with gratitude and joy. Make mine a voice of thanksgiving, Lord. And I will proclaim your name.

And when ye will offer a sacrifice of thanksgiving unto the Lord, offer it at your own will.

Leviticus 22:29

Lord, help me praise you. May I willingly and joyfully express my appreciation for your kindness. I want to offer a sacrifice of praise today. And I want to do it all day long.

He shall receive the blessing from the Lord, and righteousness from the God of his salvation.

Psalm 24:5

We can count our blessings all day, but we may forget one of the most important ones: righteousness. And that's not our righteousness, but his. Because of Christ's death on the cross, God can look at us and see him. Christ's righteousness is attributed to us. That's an amazing blessing.

God moves in a mysterious way
His wonders to perform
He plants his footsteps in the sea
And rides upon the storm.
Deep in unfathomable mines
Of never-failing skill
He treasures up his bright designs,
And works his sovereign will.
Ye fearful saints fresh courage take;
The clouds ye so much dread
Are big with mercy, and shall break
In blessings on your head.

—William Cowper, "Light Shining out of Darkness"

Know therefore that the Lord thy God, he is God, the faithful God, which keepeth covenant and mercy with them that love him and keep his commandments to a thousand generations.

Deuteronomy 7:9

I pray today to have more faith in my own abilities. I sometimes sell myself short and don't go out on a limb, afraid to fail at something even if I really want to try it. I let doubt scare me away and talk myself out of things, sure I don't have what it takes to make them happen. Then I regret never having gone after my dreams. I know that you have faith in me, but how do I find that faith for myself? Help me to recognize my own worth and strength, and to see that I am far more capable than I imagine myself to be. Help me to reach above and beyond where I am to get to where I want to be and to feel happy and fulfilled again.

And, behold, I come quickly; and my reward is with me, to give every man according as his work shall be.

Revelation 22:12

Our blessings stack up every day, innumerable and tangible. But when the Lord returns, he will bring a greater reward, a life in his presence without sorrow or pain. The day is coming. And it will be a glorious one.

And God blessed Noah and his sons, and said unto them, Be fruitful, and multiply, and replenish the earth.

Genesis 9:1

Fruitful work is a blessing, as it was after the flood. By our good works, and our children's, the earth is filled with laughter and singing. And new beginnings. No matter how you have failed, thank God for fresh starts.

The Lord shall command the blessing upon thee in thy storehouses, and in all that thou settest thine hand unto; and he shall bless thee in the land which the Lord thy God giveth thee.

Deuteronomy 28:8

Thank you, Lord, for giving me a “land,” a place, and all I need to flourish there. Your provision is constant and your strength is sufficient to make my work prosper. Fill my storehouse today with spiritual blessings I can’t count. I will praise you.

It sometimes takes a tragic event to open our eyes to the blessings that surround us. Day-to-day activities and events can seem mundane until something happens that shakes our foundation and brings into sharp focus what is truly important. Our family, friends, and communities suddenly become havens of love, support, and comfort in the midst of tragedy. Wise is the person who can see the magic and wonder in simple things without having to suffer a great loss or disaster. Happy is the person who knows that life's greatest treasures are often buried deep within the simplest things.

Now the God of hope fill you with all joy and peace in believing, that ye may abound in hope, through the power of the Holy Ghost.

Romans 15:13

Help me to remember, Lord, that your most valuable blessings are spiritual blessings: joy and peace and hope. There is power in remembering this. I receive these blessings with gratitude today.

Blessed be God, even the Father of our Lord Jesus Christ, the Father of mercies, and the God of all comfort.

2 Corinthians 1:3

We bless God, and we are blessed by him. He comforts us when we praise him and he comforts us when we need him. He is the Father of mercies. And the Father of our Lord Jesus Christ. Praise him.

May you find joy and satisfaction in your family life. In building a home and setting up a residence—be blessed! In finding a job and working diligently—be blessed! In taking care of little ones and making friends in the neighborhood—be blessed! In seeking God for all your help and guidance, bringing every care to him, yes, I pray, may you indeed be blessed.

Angels are as close as an outstretched hand, tending us in illness, worry, and dark despair. They reach for us as hands of support beneath our elbows; as hands binding up; as hands holding ours; as hands patting shoulders in encouragement and applauding efforts made toward recovery. And, when it comes to that, in hands waving us on to the distant shore where a welcoming Creator waits.

For the Lord thy God blesseth thee, as he promised thee: and thou shalt lend unto many nations, but thou shalt not borrow; and thou shalt reign over many nations, but they shall not reign over thee.

Deuteronomy 15:6

We have many blessings. And these include the freedom and security that come from his gracious provision and his ultimate authority. He provides for us, regardless of our debt. He rules in all the earth, regardless of the politics. If the nations fail and the economy collapses, he is still God. In him, then, we are truly free and completely safe. His blessings are not mere things, but attitudes about those things. In him you are safe. In him you are free.

My God, I thank you for the blessings of the single life. One of your plans was for people to get married and have children. But I know that your perfect will is also for some of us to live unmarried and not have children. For this life I thank you. For the gift to be free to learn to love without clinging. To seek relationships without owning, to offer love and kindness among many friends. Yes, Lord at times I am lonely, like all people can be. So I ask you to fill those times of emptiness with your presence. And as I continue on this path—living by myself—keep my friends and family close, no matter how far away they live. Give me peace in my work, joy in pursuit of wholeness, and comfort in solitary nights. And please continue to give me a giving heart. For I know, Lord, I am blessed.

The Lord is my rock, and my fortress, and my deliverer; my God, my strength, in whom I will trust; my buckler, and the horn of my salvation, and my high tower.

Psalm 18:2

Sometimes the blessing we need is a rock to stand on. Sometimes it is protection or strength. Often it is all of the above. Trust in God, who is your shield and high tower. He will deliver you.

Behold, happy is the man whom God correcteth: therefore despise not thou the chastening of the Almighty.

Job 5:17

Correct me today, Lord. Make me glad for the gentle but consistent voice of your Spirit, reminding me of your word and checking my temper and tongue. Make me alert to your prompting and quick to obey.

Sometimes lunchtime on the job feels like a family reunion. Our coworkers feel like family and we are grateful to belong.

What a blessing to be members of a creative, caring unit—caring about the business and those who make it happen. Productivity is up as lifted morale provides the momentum to do more and do it better, byproducts we take home.

Bless the folks down the hall, across the room, in the next department, or in the office next door. They are more than coworkers, they are workaday neighbors.

And blessed is she that believed: for there shall be a performance of those things which were told her from the Lord.

Luke 1:45

This is what her cousin Elizabeth said to the virgin Mary after an angel told her she would give birth to the Son of God. Mary believed him and was blessed. We are all blessed when we believe the promises of God, as impossible as they may seem.

May you know that a wisdom and a love transcend the things you will see and touch today. Walk in this light each step of the way. Never forget that there is more to this existence than the material side of things. And be blessed when you suddenly become aware of it: in the smile of a child, in the recognition of your own soul's existence, in the dread of death, and in the longing for immortality.

Blessed are ye, when men shall revile you, and persecute you, and shall say all manner of evil against you falsely, for my sake.

Matthew 5:11

Where in my life am I nudged by others to ignore your guidance or look the other way? Please grant me the courage to stand up for your truth, regardless of consequence.

And said unto them, Thus it is written, and thus it behooved Christ to suffer, and to rise from the dead the third day: And that repentance and remission of sins should be preached in his name among all nations, beginning at Jerusalem. And ye are witnesses of these things.

Luke 24:46–48

We weren't direct witnesses of Jesus's public ministry, death, and resurrection. But like the apostles, we are called to share the story of Jesus's saving message. Let us never forget that the mystery at the heart of our faith is meant to be shared with others.

And this is the promise that he hath promised us, even eternal life.

1 John 2:25

The Apostle John writes here to believers in the early church. They are dear to him, and he addresses them as children. As an eyewitness to the life of Jesus and the work of God, he assures them and us that "the blood of Jesus Christ his Son cleanseth us from all sin" (1 John 1:7). Eternal life is also the promise of the Gospel that bears John's name: "And this is life eternal, that they might know thee the only true God, and Jesus Christ, whom thou hast sent" (John 17:3). His reason for writing, he says, is so that you "may know that ye have eternal life" (1 John 5:13). There is certainty here, as in all the promises of God.

Blessed are the merciful: for they shall obtain mercy.

Matthew 5:7

"In calling the merciful blessed, Christ shows that true righteousness is displayed when we imitate the compassion of God, seeking to relieve the suffering of others and forgiving as we have been forgiven."

—John Calvin

How gentle are the whispers of
my guardian angel dear,

How kindly are the promptings,
ever faithful, always near;

How soft is the voice that calms
and quiets all my fear,

How peaceful is the feeling that
the road ahead is clear,

How quiet is the counsel that
my heart alone can hear.

As for me, I will behold thy face in righteousness: I shall be satisfied, when I awake, with thy likeness.

Psalm 17:15

What a blessing it is to be satisfied. And what an even greater blessing to awake in his likeness. Both come when we see his face. Scripture promises that as his children see him better they become more like him: "we know that, when he shall appear, we shall be like him; for we shall see him as he is" (1 John 3:2).

This is the future. In heaven we will be completely transformed. But there is a present sense too. The more clearly we see who God is and what he did, the more we are "conformed to the image of his Son" (Romans 8:29). This is deeply satisfying—to become more and more like Jesus. We get closer by looking at him rather than ourselves.

Bless me with silent conversations, O God, so I may be with you while doing chores, while singing in the shower, while brushing the cat. Sometimes words don't have to be spoken to be understood, and I get your message, too, in the silence that fills and comforts.

Now therefore let it please thee to bless the house of thy servant, that it may be before thee for ever: for thou blessest, O Lord, and it shall be blessed for ever.

1 Chronicles 17:27

The Lord promised David a dynasty and David was grateful. The prophet Nathan told him that God said David's would be a lasting throne. So David prays in gratitude—and reminds God of what he just said: "Therefore now, Lord, let the thing that thou hast spoken concerning thy servant and concerning his house be established for ever" (verse 23).

It is good to know the promises of God. These are the words he has spoken. And it is also good to pray the promises of God as David does here. As Irish clergyman W. C. G. Proctor explains, "The promises of God should be the basis of all our prayers. They are alike our warrant for asking and our security for receiving." Promises make great prayers.

After these things the word of the Lord came unto Abram in a vision, saying, Fear not, Abram: I am thy shield, and thy exceeding great reward.

Genesis 15:1

Abraham must have been perplexed. His nephew had chosen the "well watered" land for himself (Genesis 13:10). Furthermore, after winning a battle with other kings, Abraham had chosen to forego the spoils of war (Genesis 14:22–24). At this moment God shows up and says don't worry about the goods. I am your reward. There is more. He promises Abraham a son once more. He affirms his promise of a people and a land. But first things first. God says that he himself is the real prize. It is God that Abraham seeks, so "he believed in the Lord" (verse 6). Ultimately it is God that we seek too. He is our shield and our protector. He is our great reward.

Time may heal, Lord, but it never quite blunts loss. Thank you for the peace that is slowly seeping into my pores, allowing me to live with the unlivable; to bear the unbearable. Guide and bless my faltering steps down a new road. Prop me up when I think I can't go it alone; prod me when I tarry too long in lonely self-pity. Most of all, Kind Healer, thank you for the gifts of memory and dreams. The one comforts, the other beckons, both halves of a healing whole.

And if any man sin, we have an advocate with the Father, Jesus Christ the righteous.

1 John 2:1

Christ is both our mediator and our advocate. These are legal terms, suggesting our offenses must be accounted for. So Jesus stands between God and us, our divine lawyer before the ultimate judge. What an awesome promise then. He can do this because he is "Jesus Christ the righteous." His own sacrifices and righteousness form the basis of his appeal to the Father on our behalf. We need this assurance. His arguments are stronger than ours. And the Father always listens to the son who purchased us with his own blood.

Bless me with the kind heart of a peacemaker and a builder's sturdy hand, Lord, for these are mean-spirited, litigious times when we tear down with words and weapons first and ask questions later. Help me take every opportunity to compliment, praise, and applaud as I rebuild peace.

The Lord will give strength unto his people; the Lord will bless his people with peace.

Psalm 29:11

I'm weak today, Father. And anxious. Bills are piling up and my to-do list is getting longer. You know my relational and material struggles. So give me your strength. And peace. This promise is the blessing I need. Thank you, Father. Thank you.

While the earth remaineth, seedtime and harvest, and cold and heat, and summer and winter, and day and night shall not cease.

Genesis 8:22

God blesses us with his mercy. He tells Noah that “neither shall there any more be a flood to destroy the earth” (Genesis 9:11). The rainbow is the sign of this. “I do set my bow in the cloud, and it shall be for a token of a covenant between me and the earth” (Genesis 9:13). He does not say there will be no floods. Nor does he say there will be no judgment. He does promise he will not destroy us all at once. And seedtime and harvest shall not cease while the earth remains.

Bless those who mentor, model, and cheer
me on, Lord, urging me toward goals
I set, applauding as I reach them, and
nourishing me to try again when I don't.
Remind me to be a cheerleader. I plan
to say thanks to those who are mine.

Though I walk in the midst of trouble, thou wilt revive me: thou shalt stretch forth thine hand against the wrath of mine enemies, and thy right hand shall save me.

Psalm 138:7

We need to be revived in so many ways. Some days we need strength. Some days we need renewal of both body and soul. Revival literally means to be made alive again. Some days we certainly need that. And we find God will "revive the spirit of the humble" (Isaiah 57:15). When we acknowledge our weakness, his word can refresh us. Or correct us, if necessary. The psalmist prays, "My soul cleaveth unto the dust: quicken thou me according to thy word" (Psalm 119:25). By his word God renews nations and churches. But mostly he revives individuals who humble themselves before him. David prayed, "Create in me a clean heart, O God; and renew a right spirit within me" (Psalm 51:10). He does.

Lo, children are an heritage of the Lord: and the fruit of the womb is his reward.

Psalm 127:3

Our children are a blessing. A reward, the Psalmist says. Pray for yours today, and if you don't have any, pray for someone else's. Even if they are irritating or irrational, they are part of God's great plan. For you, and for the world.

As above the darkest storm cloud
Shines the sun, serenely bright
Waiting to restore to nature
All the glory of his light,
So, behind each cloud of sorrow,
So, in each affliction, stands,
Hid, an angel, with a blessing
From the Father in his hand.
—Daniel H. Howard

Jesus saith unto him, I am the way, the truth, and the life: no man cometh unto the Father, but by me.

John 14:6

Jesus is unequivocal here: no man comes to the Father but through him. There is no other way. No other truth. No other life. He is talking to his disciples and has just promised them a place in heaven. I'm going home and preparing a place for you, he is telling them. But you have to come through me. If you do, you will get to the Father. That's a promise.

That all the people of the earth might know the hand of the Lord, that it is mighty: that ye might fear the Lord your God for ever.

Joshua 4:24

Lord, your hand is mighty. With deep reverence, I ask for your care today, for me and those I love. Actually, I pray for all the people of the world, and that through my life, more might worship you.

All I don't know, Lord, is most apparent when children are around. Their curiosity is insatiable. I'm grateful I don't need all the answers, just a willingness to consider the questions and honor the questioners. Knock, seek, ask are imperative verbs implying your blessing on our quests.

God is our refuge and strength, a very present help in trouble.

Psalm 46:1

Our God is a very present help in trouble. Number this among the blessings you have received: rest and strength through his Spirit, whenever you call. This is a blessing indeed.

But they that wait upon the Lord shall renew their strength; they shall mount up with wings as eagles; they shall run, and not be weary; and they shall walk, and not faint.

Isaiah 40:31

When we are weak, he is strong. Better yet, when we are weak, he gives us strength. He even gives us wings. May you run today, and not faint, depending on God to renew you and bless you.

And of Benjamin he said, The beloved of the Lord shall dwell in safety by him; and the Lord shall cover him all the day long, and he shall dwell between his shoulders.

Deuteronomy 33:12

Moses says Benjamin will be beloved of the Lord. He will dwell between God's shoulders, carried or supported much like a parent carrying a child. You too are beloved of the Lord. Let him carry you today.

Lord, the only blessing I ask for these days is to restore my body to good health. When I am healthy and strong, everything else seems easier and I have the fortitude to handle challenges that come my way. Bless me with good health and vitality, and help me treat my body right and avoid stress when I can.

Each dawning of another day
She rose and said a prayer
That life would love her children
Even when she was not there.
Life has loved her children
Sometimes harshly, sometimes kind.
'Tis now I ask the blessings for
This mother who is mine.

Blessed is the man whose strength is in thee; in whose heart are the ways of them.

Psalm 84:5

Blessings abound for those who find their strength in God and have their hearts set on a spiritual journey or pilgrimage. They find support and direction, blessings in themselves as we travel life's road.

He raiseth up the poor out of the dust, and lifteth up the beggar from the dunghill, to set them among princes, and to make them inherit the throne of glory: for the pillars of the earth are the Lord's, and he hath set the world upon them.

1 Samuel 2:8

A sovereign God exalts the poor in spirit, giving them influence in his kingdom, as sons and daughters of his own. Ask the Lord to give you the humility and opportunity to act as children of a king.

We're tempted to give up until we see the geese. God provided them a "V" in which to fly, a main "point" goose providing wind resistance for followers. Geese take turns, take up slack, in the natural rhythm of things. When we ask for help, we let someone else take the point position. And we feel an updraft of air to rest in, and feel God in this current of wind.

For the mountains shall depart, and the hills be removed; but my kindness shall not depart from thee, neither shall the covenant of my peace be removed, saith the Lord that hath mercy on thee.

Isaiah 54:10

When everything around you is crumbling, God is kind, and his promises are sure. If you are having one of those days, lean into his mercy and peace. He has not left you, nor will he.

Cast thy burden upon the Lord, and he shall sustain thee: he shall never suffer the righteous to be moved.

Psalm 55:22

I need your help today, Lord. I'm carrying a lot, and my faith is a little shaky. Take my burden and my insecurity, Lord. Give me confidence and strength, dear God, and sustain me by your Spirit.

Those that be planted in the house of the Lord shall flourish in the courts of our God.

Psalm 92:13

Plant me in your house, Lord, and surround me with your people. Then I will flourish in faith, encouraged by others and strengthened by you. May the people of God be my people today.

These are mean-spirited times, and we quake and shudder. Tend us, loving Creator, and shelter us in the palm of your hand against all that would uproot and destroy us. Remind us to rejoice in your protection, for we are the flowers of your field.

And said, I cried by reason of mine affliction unto the Lord, and he heard me; out of the belly of hell cried I, and thou heardest my voice.

Jonah 2:2

This is the testimony of Jonah, in the belly of a great fish, a hell of his own making in some ways. If today you are in the belly of something, some loneliness, or sorrow, or infirmity, you too can cry out. The Lord will hear you. No matter how deep or how long your affliction, he will hear your prayer, like he did Jonah's. Even if you have run from him, as Jonah did, all you have to do is cry out. He hears the prayers of his children. And he rescues them, too.

For the Lord thy God hath blessed thee in all the works of thy hand: he knoweth thy walking through this great wilderness: these forty years the Lord thy God hath been with thee; thou hast lacked nothing.

Deuteronomy 2:7

Because of their unbelief, the children of Israel wandered 40 years in the wilderness. Yet they lacked nothing. God cares for his people, even when he requires them to do difficult things. And he blesses you, even when you are dealing with the consequences of bad choices.

My doctrine shall drop as the rain, my speech shall distil as the dew, as the small rain upon the tender herb, and as the showers upon the grass.

Deuteronomy 32:2

Nothing refreshes a parched heart like the Word of God. Like "rain upon the tender herb," the Word of God is often seen as reviving and refreshing us, bringing energy and life, as in this song of Moses.

Some blessings come in small packages! Bless this dear child, Lord, being woven from our love. It, too, is expanding like the body-cradle where the child slumbers, unknown but already loved. Bless and be with us as we practice lullabies and prayers, on our knees in joy and awe.

Likewise the Spirit also helpeth our infirmities: for we know not what we should pray for as we ought: but the Spirit itself maketh intercession for us with groanings which cannot be uttered.

Romans 8:26

When we do not know what to pray for, the Spirit of God prays for us. This is a marvelous mystery, and one we welcome. Sometimes the situation is so difficult we do not even know what we should pray for. Sometimes the choices are so murky we have no sense of what to do. In these times of discouragement and confusion, the Spirit of God takes our groaning and turns it into meaningful prayer—because God does know what we need and what we seek. The Holy Spirit then "maketh intercession for the saints according to the will of God" (verse 27). It is okay if we do not know how to pray, because thankfully, the Spirit does.

I will sing unto the Lord, because he hath dealt bountifully with me.

Psalm 13:6

Thank you, Lord. You have given me more than I deserve, pouring out your blessings and revealing your limitless love. Yes, you have dealt graciously and gently with me. I am grateful.

Angels are yet one more sign of God's goodness, a sign that God cares for us and uses many ways to express that love. Many people find peace in knowing that angels are watching.

Blessed be the Lord, because he hath heard the voice of my supplications.

Psalm 28:6

I'm grateful, God, that you hear my prayers. You heard the sadness in my voice as I prayed for a sick friend, and you heard my joy when you answered my prayer. You hear me and fill me. Blessed are you, Lord. And blessed am I.

God shall bless us; and all the ends of the earth shall fear him.

Psalm 67:7

Some days it looks like the bad guys are winning. But they are not. This truth is a blessing we seldom count, but one day all the ends of the earth shall fear him. All will see him and be awed. And of his kingdom there will be no end.

Blessed are the pure in heart:
for they shall see God.

Matthew 5:8

Pure can mean both clean and unmixed. Since your sins have been washed away by the blood of Christ, you can have a heart free of hypocrisy or guile. Ask God to give you a pure heart today. You will see him and be blessed.

But who am I, and what is my people, that we should be able to offer so willingly after this sort? for all things come of thee, and of thine own have we given thee.

1 Chronicles 29:14

Although King David would not build the temple himself, he begins to gather the materials, encouraging his people to give willingly. Consider your legacy today, as a grateful steward of God grace.

When life's winds toss me
upon the waves of uncertainty and doubt,
And when the tempest beats me
and rocks of guilt and self-pity,
When my pitiful heart yearns
for love I cannot find,
When the darkness seems darker
and the night longer,
Some unseen hand reaches down,
and with a strength and tenderness
I cannot comprehend,
Pulls me back into the light.

And I will give them one heart, and I will put a new spirit within you; and I will take the stony heart out of their flesh, and will give them an heart of flesh.

Ezekiel 11:19

God can heal a broken heart. He can also replace a stony one. In this text, his children have failed him again. They return from exile, but bring with them "detestable things" and "abominations" (verse 18). God is willing to begin again, to put a new spirit in them. Their new heart will not be perfect. It is still a heart of flesh. But that is better than a hardened heart. This he will do "that they may walk in my statutes, and keep mine ordinances, and do them: and they shall be my people, and I will be their God" (verse 20). He will soften their hearts. And he will soften ours.

Thou shalt keep therefore his statutes, and his commandments, which I command thee this day, that it may go well with thee, and with thy children after thee, and that thou mayest prolong thy days upon the earth, which the Lord thy God giveth thee, for ever.

Deuteronomy 4:40

Things work out better and last longer when God blesses us. Obey him and trust him, and for ever it will go well for you and for those you love.

For I the Lord thy God will hold thy right hand, saying unto thee, Fear not; I will help thee.

Isaiah 41:13

Help me, Lord. Hold my hand. I need to sense your presence today, steadying me as I navigate difficult relationships and conversations. I'll do better if I know you are with me. Reveal yourself, Lord, I pray.

Wherever you go, wherever you look, wherever you travel, wherever you tread—whether to the left or to the right, whether up to the sky or down to the sea—God is already there, waiting for you to arrive.

Blessed is he whose transgression is forgiven, whose sin is covered.

Psalm 32:1

Thank you, Father, that my sin is covered by the blood of Christ. So many failures, and so much grace. The blessing of your gracious forgiveness gives me hope and peace, because I am loved by you.

Behold, I have graven thee upon the palms of my hands; thy walls are continually before me.

Isaiah 49:16

By mentioning the walls of Jerusalem, critical for defense and security, God reassures his people that he has not forgotten them. He hasn't forgotten you either, and you are safe within his walls.

And said, O Lord God of Israel, there is no God like thee in the heaven, nor in the earth; which keepest covenant, and shewest mercy unto thy servants, that walk before thee with all their hearts.

2 Chronicles 6:14

Father God, despite my weakness and inconsistency, you show mercy to me, the least of your servants. Help me to walk before you with all my heart, confident in your power and in your promises.

The hand of our God is upon all them for good that seek him; but his power and his wrath is against all them that forsake him.

Ezra 8:22

Is the Lord for you or against you? Seek him, and his hand will do good for you, as you receive mercy instead of wrath and strength instead of judgment. Seen in this way, the choice is easy.

God of beasts and critters, bless them, for they bless me even when they shed on the couch and don't come when called. They love without strings and share the simplest joys of walks and catnaps, slowing me to a pace you recommend.

Ye shall have a song, as in the night when a holy solemnity is kept; and gladness of heart, as when one goeth with a pipe to come into the mountain of the Lord, to the mighty One of Israel.

Isaiah 30:29

Ours is a God who brings a song in the night (Job 35:10). But not just any song. It is the kind of song that one sings "when a holy festival is kept," a song about the greatness of our God. "And he hath put a new song in my mouth, even praise unto our God" (Psalm 40:3). Such gladness of heart is the heritage of our faith. We have a whole book of songs in scripture, and the music of the faith brings joy in our darkest hours, as Silas and Paul sang praises at midnight in a Philippian jail (Acts 16:25). Yes, you shall have a song.

Sing unto the Lord, O ye saints of his, and give thanks at the remembrance of his holiness.

Psalm 30:4

Song is the voice of a grateful heart. For this reason, many songs have been written about God's holiness and grace. Find one and sing it. And be glad, remembering and celebrating his divine perfection.

The joy of having a friend like you
is a blessing beyond compare.
Our lives are a celebration of
the special bond we share.